THE ROMAN RITUAL

revised by decree of the Second Vatican Ecumenical Council
and published by authority of Pope Paul VI

RITE OF PENANCE

Study Edition

Copyright © 1975
Publications Office
UNITED STATES CATHOLIC CONFERENCE
1312 Massachusetts Avenue, N.W.
Washington, D.C. 20005

CONTENTS

SACRED CONGREGATION FOR DIVINE WORSHIP

Prot. n. 800/73

DECREE

Reconciliation between God and men was brought about by our Lord Jesus Christ in the mystery of his death and resurrection (see Romans 5:10). The Lord entrusted the ministry of reconciliation to the Church in the person of the apostles (see 2 Corinthians 5:18ff). The Church carries this ministry out by bringing the good news of salvation to men and by baptizing them in water and the Holy Spirit (see Matthew 28:19).

Because of human weakness, Christians "turn aside from [their] early love" (see Revelation 2:4) and even break off their friendship with God by sinning. The Lord, therefore, instituted a special sacrament of penance for the pardon of sins committed after baptism (see John 20:21-23), and the Church has faithfully celebrated the sacrament throughout the centuries—in varying ways, but retaining its essential elements.

The Second Vatican Council decreed that "the rite and formulas of penance are to be revised in such a way that they may more clearly express the nature and effects of this sacrament." [1] In view of this the Congregation for Divine Worship has carefully prepared the new Rite of Penance so that the celebration of the sacrament may be more fully understood by the faithful.

In this new rite, besides the *Rite for Reconciliation of Individual Penitents,* a *Rite for Reconciliation of Several Penitents* has been drawn up to emphasize the relation of the sacrament to the community. This rite places individual confession and absolution in the context of a celebration of the word of God. Futhermore, for special occasions a *Rite for Reconciliation of Several Penitents with General Confession and Absolution* has been composed in accordance with the Pastoral Norms on General Sacramental Absolution, issued by the Congregation for the Doctrine of the Faith on June 16, 1972.[2]

The Church is solicitous in calling the faithful to continual conversion and renewal. It desires that the baptized who have sinned should acknowledge their sins against God and their neighbor and have heartfelt repentance for them, and it tries to prepare them to celebrate the sacrament of penance. For this reason the Church urges the faithful to attend penitential celebrations from time to time. This Congregation has therefore made regulations for such celebrations and has proposed examples or specimens which episcopal conferences may adapt to the needs of their own regions.

---

[1] Second Vatican Council, constitution *Sacrosanctum Concilium,* no. 72: AAS 56 (1964) 118.

[2] See AAS 64 (1964) 510-514.

Accordingly Pope Paul VI has by his authority approved the *Rite of Penance* prepared by the Congregation for Divine Worship and ordered it to be published. It is to replace the pertinent sections of the *Roman Ritual* now in use. The rite in its Latin original is to come into force as soon as it is published, but vernacular versions will be effective from the day determined by the episcopal conferences, after they have approved the translation and received confirmation from the Apostolic See.

Anything to the contrary notwithstanding.

From the office of the Congregation for Divine Worship, December 2, 1973, the First Sunday of Advent.

By special mandate of the Pope

Jean Cardinal Villot
Secretary of State

✠ Annibale Bugnini
Titular Archbishop of Diocletiana
Secretary of the Congregation for Divine Worship

RITE OF PENANCE

INTRODUCTION

I. THE MYSTERY OF RECONCILIATION IN THE HISTORY OF SALVATION

1.   The Father has shown forth his mercy by reconciling the world to himself in Christ and by making peace for all things on earth and in heaven by the blood of Christ on the cross.[1] The Son of God made man lived among men in order to free them from the slavery of sin [2] and to call them out of darkness into his wonderful light.[3] He therefore began his work on earth by preaching repentance and saying: "Turn away from sin and believe the good news" (Mark 1:15).

This invitation to repentance, which had often been sounded by the prophets, prepared the hearts of men for the coming of the Kingdom of God through the voice of John the Baptist who came "preaching a baptism of repentance for the forgiveness of sins" (Mark 1:4).

Jesus, however, not only exhorted men to repentance so that they should abandon their sins and turn wholeheartedly to the Lord,[4] but he also welcomed sinners and reconciled them with the Father.[5] Moreover, by healing the sick he signified his power to forgive sin.[6] Finally, he himself died for our sins and rose again for our justification.[7] Therefore, on the night he was betrayed and began his saving passion,[8] he instituted the sacrifice of the new covenant in his blood for the forgiveness of sins.[9] After his resurrection he sent the Holy Spirit upon the apostles, empowering them to forgive or retain sins [10] and sending them forth to all peoples to preach repentance and the forgiveness of sins in his name.[11]

The Lord said to Peter, "I will give you the keys of the kingdom of heaven, and whatever you bind on earth will be bound in heaven, and whatever you loose on earth will be loosed also in heaven" (Matthew 16:19). In obedience to this command, on the day of Pentecost Peter preached the forgiveness of sins by baptism: "Repent and let every one of you be baptized in the name of Jesus Christ for the forgiveness of your sins" (Acts 2:38).[12] Since then the Church has never failed to call men from sin to conversion and by the celebration of penance to show the victory of Christ over sin.

2.   This victory is first brought to light in baptism where our fallen nature is crucified with Christ so that the body of sin may be destroyed and we may no longer be slaves to sin, but rise with Christ and live for God.[13] For this reason the Church proclaims its faith in "the one baptism for the forgiveness of sins."

1

In the sacrifice of the Mass the passion of Christ is made present; his body given for us and his blood shed for the forgiveness of sins are offered to God again by the Church for the salvation of the world. In the eucharist Christ is present and is offered as "the sacrifice which has made our peace" [14] with God and in order that "we may be brought together in unity" [15] by his Holy Spirit.

Furthermore our Savior Jesus Christ, when he gave to his apostles and their successors power to forgive sins, instituted in his Church the sacrament of penance. Thus the faithful who fall into sin after baptism may be reconciled with God and renewed in grace.[16] The Church "possesses both water and tears: the water of baptism, the tears of penance." [17]

II. THE RECONCILIATION OF PENITENTS IN THE CHURCH'S LIFE

The Church Is Holy but Always in Need of Purification

3.   Christ "loved the Church and gave himself up for her to make her holy" (Ephesians 5:25-26), and he united the Church to himself as his bride.[18] He filled her with his divine gifts,[19] because she is his body and fullness, and through her he spreads truth and grace to all.

The members of the Church, however, are exposed to temptation and unfortunately often fall into sin. As a result, "while Christ, 'holy, innocent, and unstained' (Hebrews 7:26), did not know sin (2 Corinthians 5:21) but came only to atone for the sins of the people (see Hebrews 2:17), the Church, which includes within itself sinners and is at the same time holy and always in need of purification, constantly pursues repentance and renewal." [20]

Penance in the Church's Life and Liturgy

4.   The people of God accomplishes and perfects this continual repentance in many different ways. It shares in the sufferings of Christ [21] by enduring its own difficulties, carries out works of mercy and charity,[22] and adopts ever more fully the outlook of the Gospel message. Thus the people of God becomes in the world a sign of conversion to God. All this the Church expresses in its life and celebrates in the liturgy when the faithful confess that they are sinners and ask pardon of God and of their brothers and sisters. This happens in penitential services, in the proclamation of the word of God, in prayer, and in the penitential aspects of the eucharistic celebration.[23]

In the sacrament of penance the faithful "obtain from the mercy of God pardon for their sins against him; at the same time they are reconciled with the Church which they wounded by their sins and which works for their conversion by charity, example, and prayer." [24]

Reconciliation with God and with the Church

5.   Since every sin is an offense against God which disrupts our friendship with him, "the ultimate purpose of penance is that we should love God deeply and commit ourselves completely to him." [25] Therefore, the sinner who by the grace of a merciful God embraces the way of penance comes back to the Father who "first loved us" (1 John 4:19), to Christ

2

who gave himself up for us,[26] and to the Holy Spirit who has been poured out on us abundantly.[27]

"By the hidden and loving mystery of God's design men are joined together in the bonds of supernatural solidarity, so much so that the sin of one harms the others just as the holiness of one benefits the others." [28] Penance always entails reconciliation with our brothers and sisters who are always harmed by our sins.

In fact, men frequently join together to commit injustice. It is thus only fitting that they should help each other in doing penance so that freed from sin by the grace of Christ they may work with all men of good will for justice and peace in the world.

The Sacrament of Penance and Its Parts

6.   The follower of Christ who has sinned but who has been moved by the Holy Spirit to come to the sacrament of penance should above all be converted to God with his whole heart. This inner conversion of heart embraces sorrow for sin and the intent to lead a new life. It is expressed through confession made to the Church, due satisfaction, and amendment of life. God grants pardon for sin through the Church, which works by the ministry of priests.[29]

A.   Contrition

The most important act of the penitent is contrition, which is "heartfelt sorrow and aversion for the sin committed along with the intention of sinning no more." [30] "We can only approach the Kingdom of Christ by *metanoia*. This is a profound change of the whole person by which one begins to consider, judge, and arrange his life according to the holiness and love of God, made manifest in his Son in the last days and given to us in abundance" (see Hebrews 1:2, Colossians 1:19 and *passim*).[31] The genuineness of penance depends on this heartfelt contrition. For conversion should affect a person from within so that it may progressively enlighten him and render him continually more like Christ.

B.   Confession

The sacrament of penance includes the confession of sins, which comes from true knowledge of self before God and from contrition for those sins. However, this inner examination of heart and the exterior accusation should be made in the light of God's mercy. Confession requires in the penitent the will to open his heart to the minister of God, and in the minister a spiritual judgment by which, acting in the person of Christ, he pronounces his decision of forgiveness or retention of sins in accord with the power of the keys.[32]

C.   Act of Penance (Satisfaction)

True conversion is completed by acts of penance or satisfaction for the sins committed, by amendment of conduct, and also by the reparation of injury.[33] The kind and extent of the satisfaction should be suited to the personal condition of each penitent so that each one may restore the order which he disturbed and through the corresponding remedy be cured of the sickness from which he suffered. Therefore, it is necessary that the act of penance really be a remedy for sin and a help to renewal of life. Thus the penitent, "forgetting the things which are behind him" (Philippians 3:13), again becomes part of the mystery of salvation and turns himself toward the future.

D. Absolution

Through the sign of absolution God grants pardon to the sinner who in sacramental confession manifests his change of heart to the Church's minister, and thus the sacrament of penance is completed. In God's design the humanity and loving kindness of our Savior have visibly appeared to us,[34] and God uses visible signs to give salvation and to renew the broken covenant.

In the sacrament of penance the Father receives the repentant son who comes back to him, Christ places the lost sheep on his shoulders and brings it back to the sheepfold, and the Holy Spirit sanctifies this temple of God again or lives more fully within it. This is finally expressed in a renewed and more fervent sharing of the Lord's table, and there is great joy at the banquet of God's Church over the son who has returned from afar.[35]

The Necessity and Benefit of the Sacrament

7. Just as the wound of sin is varied and multiple in the life of individuals and of the community, so too the healing which penance provides is varied. Those who by grave sin have withdrawn from the communion of love with God are called back in the sacrament of penance to the life they have lost. And those who through daily weakness fall into venial sins draw strength from a repeated celebration of penance to gain the full freedom of the children of God.

a) To obtain the saving remedy of the sacrament of penance, according to the plan of our merciful God, the faithful must confess to a priest each and every grave sin which they remember upon examination of their conscience.[36]

b) Moreover, frequent and careful celebration of this sacrament is also very useful as a remedy for venial sins. This is not a mere ritual repetition or psychological exercise, but a serious striving to perfect the grace of baptism so that, as we bear in our body the death of Jesus Christ, his life may be seen in us ever more clearly.[37] In confession of this kind, penitents who accuse themselves of venial faults should try to conform more closely to Christ and to follow the voice of the Spirit more attentively.

In order that this sacrament of healing may truly achieve its purpose among Christ's faithful, it must take root in their whole lives and move them to more fervent service of God and neighbor.

The celebration of this sacrament is thus always an act in which the Church proclaims its faith, gives thanks to God for the freedom with which Christ has made us free,[38] and offers its life as a spiritual sacrifice in praise of God's glory, as it hastens to meet the Lord Jesus.

4

III. OFFICES AND MINISTRIES IN THE RECONCILIATION OF PENITENTS

The Community in the Celebration of Penance

8. The whole Church, as a priestly people, acts in different ways in the work of reconciliation which has been entrusted to it by the Lord. Not only does the Church call sinners to repentance by preaching the word of God, but it also intercedes for them and helps penitents with maternal care and solicitude to acknowledge and admit their sins and so obtain the mercy of God who alone can forgive sins. Furthermore, the Church becomes the instrument of the conversion and absolution of the penitent through the ministry entrusted by Christ to the apostles and their successors.[39]

9. The Minister of the Sacrament of Penance

a) The Church exercises the ministry of the sacrament of penance through bishops and presbyters. By preaching God's word they call the faithful to conversion; in the name of Christ and by the power of the Holy Spirit they declare and grant the forgiveness of sins.

In the exercise of this ministry presbyters act in communion with the bishop and share in his power and office of regulating the penitential discipline.[40]

b) The competent minister of the sacrament of penance is a priest who has the faculty to absolve in accordance with canon law. All priests, however, even though not approved to hear confessions, absolve validly and licitly all penitents who are in danger of death.

10. The Pastoral Exercise of This Ministry

a) In order to fulfill his ministry properly and faithfully the confessor should understand the disorders of souls and apply the appropriate remedies to them. He should fulfill his office of judge wisely and should acquire the knowledge and prudence necessary for this task by serious study, guided by the teaching authority of the Church and especially by fervent prayer to God. Discernment of spirits is a deep knowledge of God's action in the hearts of men; it is a gift of the Spirit as well as the fruit of charity.[41]

b) The confessor should always be ready and willing to hear the confessions of the faithful when they make a reasonable request of him.[42]

c) By receiving the repentant sinner and leading him to the light of the truth the confessor fulfills a paternal function: he reveals the heart of the Father and shows the image of Christ the Good Shepherd. He should keep in mind that he has been entrusted with the ministry of Christ, who mercifully accomplished the saving work of man's redemption and who is present by his power in the sacraments.[43]

d) As the minister of God the confessor comes to know the secrets of another's conscience, and he is bound to keep the sacramental seal of confession absolutely inviolate.

The Penitent

11.   The acts of the penitent in the celebration of the sacrament are of the greatest importance.

When with proper dispositions he approaches this saving remedy instituted by Christ and confesses his sins, he shares by his actions in the sacrament itself; the sacrament is completed when the words of absolution are spoken by the minister in the name of Christ.

Thus the faithful Christian, as he experiences and proclaims the mercy of God in his life, celebrates with the priest the liturgy by which the Church continually renews itself.

IV.   THE CELEBRATION OF THE SACRAMENT OF PENANCE

The Place of Celebration

12.   The sacrament of penance is celebrated in the place and location prescribed by law.

The Time of Celebration

13.   The reconciliation of penitents may be celebrated at any time on any day, but it is desirable that the faithful know the day and time at which the priest is available for this ministry. They should be encouraged to approach the sacrament of penance at times when Mass is not being celebrated and especially during the scheduled periods.[44]

The season of Lent is most appropriate for celebrating the sacrament of penance. Already on Ash Wednesday the people of God has heard the solemn invitation "Turn away from sin and believe the good news." It is therefore fitting to have several penitential celebrations during Lent, so that all the faithful may have an opportunity to be reconciled with God and their neighbor and so be able to celebrate the paschal mystery in the Easter triduum with renewed hearts.

Liturgical Vestments

14.   The regulations laid down by the local Ordinaries for the use of liturgical vestments in the celebration of penance are to be observed.

A.   Rite for the Reconciliation of Individual Penitents

Preparation of Priest and Penitent

15.   Priest and penitent should first prepare themselves by prayer to celebrate the sacrament. The priest should call upon the Holy Spirit so that he may receive enlightenment and charity. The penitent should compare his life with the example and commandments of Christ and then pray to God for the forgiveness of his sins.

Welcoming the Penitent

16.   The priest should welcome the penitent with fraternal charity and, if the occasion permits, address him with friendly words. The penitent then makes the sign of the cross, saying: "In the name of the Father and

of the Son and of the Holy Spirit. Amen." The priest may also make the sign of the cross with the penitent. Next the priest briefly urges the penitent to have confidence in God. If the penitent is unknown to the priest, it is proper for him to indicate his state in life, the time of his last confession, his difficulties in leading the Christian life, and anything else which may help the confessor in exercising his ministry.

Reading the Word of God

17. Then the priest, or the penitent himself, may read a text of holy Scripture, or this may be done as part of the preparation for the sacrament. Through the word of God the Christian receives light to recognize his sins and is called to conversion and to confidence in God's mercy.

Confession of Sins and the Act of Penance

18. The penitent then confesses his sins, beginning, where customary, with a form of general confession: *I confess to almighty God.* If necessary, the priest should help the penitent to make a complete confession; he should also encourage him to have sincere sorrow for his sins against God. Finally, the priest should offer suitable counsel to help the penitent begin a new life and, where necessary, instruct him in the duties of the Christian way of life.

If the penitent has been the cause of harm or scandal to others, the priest should lead him to resolve that he will make appropriate restitution.

Then the priest imposes an act of penance or satisfaction on the penitent; this should serve not only to make up for the past but also to help him to begin a new life and provide him with an antidote to weakness. As far as possible, the penance should correspond to the seriousness and nature of the sins. This act of penance may suitably take the form of prayer, self-denial, and especially service of one's neighbor and works of mercy. These will underline the fact that sin and its forgiveness have a social aspect.

The Prayer of the Penitent and the Absolution by the Priest

19. After this the penitent manifests his contrition and resolution to begin a new life by means of a prayer for God's pardon. It is desirable that this prayer should be based on the words of Scripture.

Following this prayer, the priest extends his hands, or at least his right hand, over the head of the penitent and pronounces the formula of absolution, in which the essential words are: "I absolve you from your sins in the name of the Father and of the Son and of the Holy Spirit." As he says the final words the priest makes the sign of the cross over the penitent. The form of absolution (see no. 46) indicates that the reconciliation of the penitent comes from the mercy of the Father; it shows the connection between the reconciliation of the sinner and the paschal mystery of Christ; it stresses the role of the Holy Spirit in the forgiveness of sins; finally, it underlines the ecclesial aspect of the sacrament because reconciliation with God is asked for and given through the ministry of the Church.

7

Proclamation of Praise and Dismissal of the Penitent

20.   After receiving pardon for his sins the penitent praises the mercy of God and gives him thanks in a short invocation taken from scripture. Then the priest tells him to go in peace.

The penitent continues his conversion and expresses it by a life renewed according to the Gospel and more and more steeped in the love of God, for "love covers over a multitude of sins" (1 Peter 4:8).

Short Rite

21.   When pastoral need dictates it, the priest may omit or shorten some parts of the rite but must always retain in their entirety the confession of sins and the acceptance of the act of penance, the invitation to contrition (no. 44), and the form of absolution and the dismissal. In imminent danger of death, it is sufficient for the priest to say the essential words of the form of absolution, namely, "I absolve you from your sins in the name of the Father, and of the Son, and of the Holy Spirit."

B.   Rite for Reconciliation of Several Penitents with Individual Confession and Absolution

22.   When a number of penitents assemble at the same time to receive sacramental reconciliation, it is fitting that they be prepared for the sacrament by a celebration of the word of God.

Those who will receive the sacrament at another time may also take part in the service.

Communal celebration shows more clearly the ecclesial nature of penance. The faithful listen together to the word of God, which proclaims his mercy and invites them to conversion; at the same time they examine the conformity of their lives with that word of God and help each other through common prayer. After each person has confessed his sins and received absolution, all praise God together for his wonderful deeds on behalf of the people he has gained for himself through the blood of his Son.

If necessary, several priests should be available in suitable places to hear individual confessions and to reconcile the penitents.

Introductory Rites

23.   When the faithful are assembled, a suitable hymn may be sung. Then the priest greets them, and, if necessary, he or another minister gives a brief introduction to the celebration and explains the order of service. Next he invites all to pray and after a period of silence completes the (opening) prayer.

The Celebration of the Word of God

24.   The sacrament of penance should begin with a hearing of God's word, because through his word God calls men to repentance and leads them to a true conversion of heart.

One or more readings may be chosen. If more than one are read, a psalm, another suitable song, or a period of silence should be inserted between them, so that the word of God may be more deeply understood and heartfelt assent may be given to it. If there is only one reading, it is preferable that it be from the gospel.

Readings should be chosen which illustrate the following:

a) the voice of God calling men back to conversion and ever closer conformity with Christ;

b) the mystery of our reconciliation through the death and resurrection of Christ and through the gift of the Holy Spirit;

c) the judgment of God about good and evil in men's lives as a help in the examination of conscience.

25. The homily, taking its theme from the scriptural text, should lead the penitents to examine their consciences and to turn away from sin and toward God. It should remind the faithful that sin works against God, against the community and one's neighbors, and against the sinner himself. Therefore, it would be good to recall:

a) the infinite mercy of God, greater than all our sins, by which again and again he calls us back to himself;

b) the need for interior repentance, by which we are genuinely prepared to make reparation for sin;

c) the social aspect of grace and sin, by which the actions of individuals in some degree affect the whole body of the Church;

d) the duty to make satisfaction for sin, which is effective because of Christ's work of reparation and requires especially, in addition to works of penance, the exercise of true charity toward God and neighbor.

26. After the homily a suitable period of silence should be allowed for examining one's conscience and awakening true contrition for sin. The priest or a deacon or other minister may help the faithful with brief considerations or a litany, adapted to their background, age, etc.

If it is judged suitable, this communal examination of conscience and awakening of contrition may take the place of the homily. But in this case it should be clearly based on the text of scripture that has just been read.

The Rite of Reconciliation

27. At the invitation of the deacon or other minister, all kneel or bow their heads and say a form of general confession (for example, *I confess to almighty God*). Then they stand and join in a litany or suitable song to express confession of sins, heartfelt contrition, prayer for forgiveness, and trust in God's mercy. Finally, they say the Lord's Prayer, which is never omitted.

28. After the Lord's Prayer the priests go to the places assigned for confession. The penitents who desire to confess their sins go to the priest of their choice. After receiving a suitable act of penance, they are absolved by him with the form for the reconciliation of an individual penitent.

9

29.   When the confessions are over, the priests return to the sanctuary. The priest who presides invites all to make an act of thanksgiving and to praise God for his mercy. This may be done in a psalm or hymn or litany. Finally, the priest concludes the celebration with prayer, praising God for the great love he has shown us.

Dismissal of the People

30.   After the prayer of thanksgiving the priest blesses the faithful. Then the deacon or the priest himself dismisses the congregation.

C.   Rite for Reconciliation of Penitents with
General Confession and Absolution

The Discipline of General Absolution

31.   Individual, integral confession and absolution remain the only ordinary way for the faithful to reconcile themselves with God and the Church, unless physical or moral impossibility excuses from this kind of confession.

Particular, occasional circumstances may render it lawful and even necessary to give general absolution to a number of penitents without their previous individual confession.

In addition to cases involving danger of death, it is lawful to give sacramental absolution to several of the faithful at the same time, after they have made only a generic confession but have been suitably called to repentance, if there is grave need, namely when, in view of the number of penitents, sufficient confessors are not available to hear individual confessions properly within a suitable period of time, so that the penitents would, through no fault of their own, have to go without sacramental grace or holy communion for a long time. This may happen especially in mission territories but in other places as well and also in groups of persons when the need is established.

General absolution is not lawful, when confessors are available, for the sole reason of the large number of penitents, as may be on the occasion of some major feast or pilgrimage.[45]

32.   The judgment about the presence of the above conditions and the decision concerning the lawfulness of giving general sacramental absolution are reserved to the bishop of the diocese, who is to consult with the other members of the episcopal conference.

Over and above the cases determined by the diocesan bishop, if any other serious need arises for giving sacramental absolution to several persons together, the priest must have recourse to the local Ordinary beforehand, when this is possible, if he is to give absolution lawfully. Otherwise, he should inform the Ordinary as soon as possible of the need and of the absolution which he gave.[46]

33.   In order that the faithful may profit from sacramental absolution given to several persons at the same time, it is absolutely necessary that they be properly disposed. Each one should be sorry for his sins and resolve to avoid committing them again. He should intend to repair any

10

scandal and harm he may have caused and likewise resolve to confess in due time each one of the grave sins which he cannot confess at present. These dispositions and conditions, which are required for the validity of the sacrament, should be carefully recalled to the faithful by priests.[47]

34.   Those who receive pardon for grave sins by a common absolution should go to individual confession before they receive this kind of absolution again, unless they are impeded by a just reason. They are strictly bound, unless this is morally impossible, to go to confession within a year. The precept which obliges each of the faithful to confess at least once a year to a priest all the grave sins which he has not individually confessed before also remains in force in this case too.[48]

The Rite of General Absolution

35.   For the reconciliation of penitents by general confession and absolution in the cases provided by law, everything takes place as described above for the reconciliation of several penitents with individual confession and absolution, with the following exceptions:

a) After the homily or during it, the faithful who seek general absolution should be instructed to dispose themselves properly, that is, each one should be sorry for his sins and resolve to avoid committing them again. He should intend to repair any scandal and harm he may have caused and likewise resolve to confess in due time each one of the grave sins which cannot be confessed at present.[49] Some act of penance should be proposed for all; individuals may add to this penance if they wish.

b) The deacon, another minister, or the priest then calls upon the penitents who wish to receive absolution to show their intention by some sign (for example, by bowing their heads, kneeling, or giving some other sign determined by the episcopal conferences). They should also say together a form of general confession (for example, *I confess to almighty God*), which may be followed by a litany or a penitential song. Then the Lord's Prayer is sung or said by all, as indicated in no. 27, above.

c) Then the priest calls upon the grace of the Holy Spirit for the forgiveness of sins, proclaims the victory over sin of Christ's death and resurrection, and gives sacramental absolution to the penitents.

d) Finally, the priest invites the people to give thanks, as described in no. 29, above, and, omitting the concluding prayer, he immediately blesses and dismisses them.

V.   PENITENTIAL CELEBRATIONS

Nature and Structure

36.   Penitential celebrations are gatherings of the people of God to hear the proclamation of God's word. This invites them to conversion and renewal of life and announces our freedom from sin through the death and resurrection of Christ. The structure of these services is the same as that usually followed in celebrations of the word of God [50] and given in the *Rite for Reconciliation of Several Penitents.*

11

It is appropriate, therefore, that after the introductory rites (song, greeting, and prayer) one or more biblical readings be chosen with songs, psalms, or periods of silence inserted between them. In the homily these readings should be explained and applied to the congregation. Before or after the readings from scripture, readings from the Fathers or other writers may be selected which will help the community and each person to a true awareness of sin and heartfelt sorrow, in other words, to bring about conversion of life.

After the homily and reflection on God's word, it is desirable that the congregation, united in voice and spirit, pray together in a litany or in some other way suited to general participation. At the end the Lord's Prayer is said, asking God our Father "to forgive us our sins as we forgive those who sin against us . . . and deliver us from evil." The priest or the minister who presides concludes with a prayer and the dismissal of the people.

Benefit and Importance

37.   Care should be taken that the faithful do not confuse these celebrations with the celebration of the sacrament of penance.[51] Penitential celebrations are very helpful in promoting conversion of life and purification of heart.[52]

It is desirable to arrange such services especially for these purposes:

—to foster the spirit of penance within the Christian community;

—to help the faithful to prepare for confession which can be made individually later at a convenient time;

—to help children gradually to form their conscience about sin in human life and about freedom from sin through Christ;

—to help catechumens during their conversion.

Penitential celebrations, moreover, are very useful in places where no priest is available to give sacramental absolution. They offer help in reaching that perfect contrition which comes from charity and enables the faithful to attain to God's grace through a desire for the sacrament of penance.[53]

VI.   ADAPTATIONS OF THE RITE TO VARIOUS REGIONS AND CIRCUMSTANCES

Adaptations by the Episcopal Conferences

38.   In preparing particular rituals episcopal conferences may adapt the rite of penance to the needs of individual regions so that after confirmation by the Apostolic See the rituals may be used in the respective regions. It is the responsibility of episcopal conferences in this matter:

a) to establish regulations for the discipline of the sacrament of penance, particularly those affecting the ministry of priests and the reservation of sins;

12

b) to determine more precise regulations about the place proper for the ordinary celebration of the sacrament of penance and about the signs of penance to be shown by the faithful before general absolution (see no. 35, above);

c) to prepare translations of texts adapted to the character and language of each people and also to compose new texts for the prayers of the faithful and the minister, keeping intact the sacramental form.

The Competence of the Bishop

39. It is for the diocesan bishop:

a) to regulate the discipline of penance in his diocese,[54] including adaptations of the rite according to the rules proposed by the episcopal conference;

b) to determine, after consultation with the other members of the episcopal conference, when general sacramental absolution may be permitted under the conditions laid down by the Holy See.[55]

Adaptations by the Minister

40. It is for priests, and especially parish priests:

a) in reconciling individuals or the community, to adapt the rite to the concrete circumstances of the penitents. The essential structure and the entire form of absolution must be kept, but if necessary they may omit some parts for pastoral reasons or enlarge upon them, may select the texts of readings or prayers, and may choose a place more suitable for the celebration according to the regulations of the episcopal conference, so that the entire celebration may be rich and fruitful;

b) to propose and prepare occasional penitential celebrations during the year, especially in Lent. In order that the texts chosen and the order of the celebration may be adapted to the conditions and circumstances of the community or group (for example, children, sick persons, etc.), they may be assisted by others, including the laity;

c) to decide to give general sacramental absolution preceded by only a generic confession, when a grave necessity not foreseen by the diocesan bishop arises and when recourse to him is not possible. They are obliged to notify the Ordinary as soon as possible of the need and of the fact that absolution was given.

[1] See 2 Corinthians 5:18ff; Colossians 1:20.
[2] See John 8:34-36.
[3] See 1 Peter 2:9.
[4] See Luke 15.
[5] Luke 5:20, 27-32; 7:48.
[6] See Matthew 9:2-8.
[7] See Romans 4:25.
[8] See Roman Missal, Eucharistic Prayer III.
[9] See Matthew 26:28.
[10] See John 20:19-23.
[11] See Luke 24:47.
[12] See Acts 3:19, 26; 17:30.
[13] See Romans 6:4-10.
[14] Roman Missal, Eucharistic Prayer III.
[15] Roman Missal, Eucharistic Prayer II.
[16] See Council of Trent, Session XIV, De sacramento Paenitentiae, Chapter I: Denz.-Schön. 1668 and 1670: can. 1; Denz.-Schön. 1701.
[17] St. Ambrose, Letter 41:12: PL 16, 1116.
[18] See Revelation 19:7.
[19] See Ephesians 1:22-23; Second Vatican Council, constitution Lumen gentium, no. 7: AAS 57 (1965) 9-11.
[20] Second Vatican Council, constitution, Lumen gentium, no. 8: ibid., 12.
[21] See 1 Peter 4:13.
[22] See 1 Peter 4:8.
[23] See Council of Trent, Session XIV, De sacramento Paenitentiae: Denz.-Schön. 1638, 1740, 1743; Congregation of Rites, instruction Eucharisticum mysterium, May 25, 1967, no. 35: AAS 59 (1967) 560-561; Roman Missal, General Instruction, nos. 29, 30, 56 a. b. g.
[24] Second Vatican Council, constitution Lumen gentium, no. 11: AAS 57 (1965) 15-16.
[25] Paul VI, Apostolic Constitution Paenitemini, February 17, 1966: AAS 58 (1966) 179; See Second Vatican Council, constitution Lumen gentium, no. 11: AAS 57 (1965) 15-16.
[26] See Galatians 2:20, Ephesians 5:25.
[27] See Titus 3:6.
[28] Paul VI, Apostolic Constitution Indulgentiarum doctrina, January 1, 1967, no. 4: AAS 59 (1967) 9; see Pius XII, encyclical Mystici Corporis, June 29, 1943: AAS 35 (1943) 213.
[29] See Council of Trent, Session XIV, De sacramento Paenitentiae, Chapter I: Denz.-Schön. 1673-1675.
[30] Ibid., Chapter 4: Denz.-Schön. 1676.
[31] Paul VI, Apostolic Constitution Paenitemini, February 17, 1966: AAS 58 (1966) 179.
[32] See Council of Trent, Session XIV, De sacramento Paenitentiae, Chapter 5: Denz.-Schön. 1679.
[33] See Council of Trent, Session XIV, De sacramento Paenitentiae, Chapter 8: Denz.-Schön. 1690-1692; Paul VI, Apostolic Constitution Indulgentiarum doctrina, January 1, 1967, nos. 2-3: AAS 59 (1967) 6-8.
[34] See Titus 3:4-5.
[35] See Luke 15:7, 10, 32.
[36] See Council of Trent, Session XIV, De sacramento Paenitentiae, can. 7-8: Denz.-Schön. 1707-1708.
[37] See 2 Corinthians 4:10.
[38] See Galatians 4:31.
[39] See Matthew 18:18; John 20:23.

[40] See Second Vatican Council, constitution *Lumen gentium*, no. 26: AAS 57 (1965) 31-32.

[41] See Philippians 1:9-10.

[42] See Congregation for the Doctrine of the Faith, *Normae pastorales circa absolutionem sacramentalem generali modo impertiendam*, June 16, 1972, No. XII: AAS 64 (1972) 514.

[43] See Second Vatican Council, constitution *Sacrosanctum Concilium*, no. 7: AAS 56 (1964) 100-101.

[44] See Congregation of Rites, instruction *Eucharisticum mysterium*, May 25, 1967, no. 35: AAS 59 (1967) 560-561.

[45] Congregation for the Doctrine of the Faith, *Normae pastorales circa absolutionem sacramentalem generali modo impertiendam*, June 16, 1972, no. III: AAS 64 (1972) 511.

[46] *Ibid.*, no. V: *loc. cit.*, 512.

[47] *Ibid.*, nos. VI and XI: *loc. cit.*, 512, 514

[48] *Ibid.*, nos. VII and VIII: *loc. cit.*, 512-513.

[49] See *Ibid.*, no. VI: *loc. cit.*, 512.

[50] See Congregation of Rites, instruction *Inter Oecumenici*, September 26, 1964, nos. 37-39: AAS 50 (1964) 110-111.

[51] See Congregation for the Doctrine of the Faith, *Normae pastorales circa absolutionem sacramentalem generali modo impertiendam*, June 16, 1972, no. X: AAS 64 (1972) 513-514.

[52] *Ibid.*

[53] See Council of Trent, Session XIV, *De sacramento Paenitentiae*, chapter 5: Denz.-Schön. 1677.

[54] See Second Vatican Council, constitution *Lumen gentium*, no. 26: AAS 57 (1965) 31-32.

[55] See Congregation for the Doctrine of the Faith, *Normae pastorales circa absolutionem sacramentalem generali modo impertiendam*, no. V: AAS 64 (1972), 512.

CHAPTER I

RITE FOR RECONCILIATION
OF INDIVIDUAL PENITENTS

RECEPTION OF THE PENITENT

41.   When the penitent comes to confess his sins, the priest welcomes him warmly and greets him with kindness.

42.   Then the penitent makes the sign of the cross which the priest may make also.

In the name of the Father, and of the Son, and of the Holy Spirit. Amen.

The priest invites the penitent to have trust in God, in these or similar words:

May God, who has enlightened every heart,
help you to know your sins
and trust in his mercy.

℞.   **Amen.**

Or: [67]

The Lord does not wish the sinner to die
but to turn back to him and live.
Come before him with trust in his mercy.   (Ezekiel 33:11)

Or: [68]

May the Lord Jesus welcome you.
He came to call sinners, not the just.
Have confidence in him.   (Luke 5:32)

Or: [69]

May the grace of the Holy Spirit
fill your heart with light,
that you may confess your sins with loving trust
and come to know that God is merciful.

17

Or: [70]

May the Lord be in your heart
and help you to confess your sins with true sorrow.

Or: [71]

If you have sinned, do not lose heart.
We have Jesus Christ to plead for us with the Father:
he is the holy One,
the atonement for our sins
and for the sins of the whole world.   (1 John 2:1-2)

READING OF THE WORD OF GOD (Optional)

43.   Then the priest may read or say from memory a text of Scripture
which proclaims God's mercy and calls man to conversion.

Let us look on Jesus   [72]
who suffered to save us
and rose again for our justification.

Isaiah 53:4-6

It was our infirmities that he bore,
our sufferings that he endured,
While we thought of him as stricken,
as one smitten by God and afflicted.
But he was pierced for our offenses,
crushed for our sins,
Upon him was the chastisement that
makes us whole,
by his stripes we were healed.
We had all gone astray like sheep,
each following his own way;
But the Lord laid upon him
the guilt of us all.

Or: [73]

Ezekiel 11:19-20

Let us listen to the Lord as he speaks to us:

I will give them a new heart and put a new spirit within them;
I will remove the stony heart from their bodies, and replace it
with a natural heart, so that they will live according to my
statutes, and observe and carry out my ordinances; thus they
shall be my people and I will be their God.

18

Or: [74]
Matthew 6:14-15

Let us listen to the Lord as he speaks to us:

If you forgive the faults of others, your heavenly Father will forgive you yours. If you do not forgive others, neither will your Father forgive you.

Or: [75]
Mark: 1:14-15

After John's arrest, Jesus appeared in Galilee proclaiming the good news of God: "This is the time of fulfillment. The reign of God is at hand! Reform your lives and believe in the gospel!"

Or: [76]
Luke 6:31-38

Let us listen to the Lord as he speaks to us:

Do to others what you would have them do to you. If you love those who love you, what credit is that to you? Even sinners love those who love them. If you do good to those who do good to you, how can you claim any credit? Sinners do as much. If you lend to those from whom you expect repayment, what merit is there in it for you? Even sinners lend to sinners, expecting to be repaid in full.

Love your enemy and do good; lend without expecting repayment. Then will your recompense be great. You will rightly be called sons of the Most High, since he himself is good to the ungrateful and the wicked.

Be compassionate, as your Father is compassionate. Do not judge, and you will not be judged. Do not condemn, and you will not be condemned. Pardon, and you shall be pardoned. Give, and it shall be given to you. Good measure pressed down, shaken together, running over, will they pour into the fold of your garment. For the measure you measure with will be measured back to you.

Or: [77]
Luke 15:1-7

The tax collectors and sinners were all gathering around to hear him, at which the Pharisees and the scribes murmured, "This man welcomes sinners and eats with them." Then he addressed this parable to them: "Who among you, if he has a hundred

19

sheep and loses one of them, does not leave the ninety-nine in the wasteland and follow the lost one until he finds it? And when he finds it, he puts it on his shoulders in jubilation. Once arrived home, he invites friends and neighbors in and says to them, 'Rejoice with me because I have found my lost sheep.' I tell you, there will likewise be more joy in heaven over one repentant sinner than over ninety-nine righteous people who have no need to repent.

Or: [78]

John 20:19-23

On the evening of that first day of the week, even though the disciples had locked the doors of the place where they were for fear of the Jews, Jesus came and stood before them. "Peace be with you," he said. When he had said this, he showed them his hands and his side. At the sight of the Lord the disciples rejoiced. "Peace be with you," he said again.

"As the Father has sent me,
so I send you."

Then he breathed on them and said:

"Receive the Holy Spirit.
If you forgive men's sins,
they are forgiven them;
if you hold them bound,
they are held bound."

Or: [79]

Romans 5:8-9

It is precisely in this that God proves his love for us: that while we were still sinners, Christ died for us. Now that we have been justified by his blood, it is all the more certain that we shall be saved by him from God's wrath.

Or: [80]

Ephesians 5:1-2

Be imitators of God as his dear children. Follow the way of love, even as Christ loved you. He gave himself for us as an offering to God, a gift of pleasing fragrance.

Or: [81]
  Colossians 1:12-14

Give thanks to the Father for having made you worthy to share
the lot of the saints in light. He rescued us from the power of
darkness and brought us into the kingdom of his beloved Son.
Through him we have redemption, the forgiveness of our sins.

Or: [82]
  Colossians 3:8-10, 12-17

You must put that aside now: all the anger and quick temper,
the malice, the insults, the foul language. Stop lying to one
another. What you have done is put aside your old self with its
past deeds and put on a new man, one who grows in knowledge
as he is formed anew in the image of his Creator.

Because you are God's chosen ones, holy and beloved, clothe
yourselves with heartfelt mercy, with kindness, humility, meekness, and patience. Bear with one another; forgive whatever
grievances you have against one another. Forgive as the Lord
has forgiven you. Over all these virtues put on love, which binds
the rest together and makes them perfect. Christ's peace must
reign in your hearts, since as members of the one body you have
been called to that peace. Dedicate yourselves to thankfulness.

Let the word of Christ, rich as it is, dwell in you. In wisdom
made perfect, instruct and admonish one another. Sing gratefully to God from your hearts in psalms, hymns, and inspired
songs. Whatever you do, whether in speech or in action, do it
in the name of the Lord Jesus. Give thanks to God the Father
through him.

Or: [83]
  1 John 1:6-7,9

If we say, "We have fellowship with him,"
while continuing to walk in darkness,
we are liars and do not act in truth.
But if we walk in light,
as he is in the light,
we have fellowship with one another,
and the blood of his Son Jesus cleanses us
from all sin.

But if we acknowledge our sins,
he who is just can be trusted
to forgive our sins
and cleanse us from every wrong.

A reading may also be chosen from those given in nos. 101-201 for the reconciliation of several penitents. The priest and penitent may choose other readings from scripture.

CONFESSION OF SINS AND ACCEPTANCE OF SATISFACTION

44.   Where it is the custom, the penitent says a general formula for confession (for example, *I confess to almighty God*) before he confesses his sins.

If necessary, the priest helps the penitent to make an integral confession and gives him suitable counsel. He urges him to be sorry for his faults, reminding him that through the sacrament of penance the Christian dies and rises with Christ and is thus renewed in the paschal mystery. The priest proposes an act of penance which the penitent accepts to make satisfaction for sin and to amend his life.

The priest should make sure that he adapts his counsel to the penitent's circumstances.

PRAYER OF THE PENITENT

45.   The priest then asks the penitent to express his sorrow, which the penitent may do in these or similar words:

My God,
I am sorry for my sins with all my heart.
In choosing to do wrong
and failing to do good,
I have sinned against you
whom I should love above all things.
I firmly intend, with your help,
to do penance,
to sin no more,
and to avoid whatever leads me to sin.
Our Savior Jesus Christ
suffered and died for us.
In his name, my God, have mercy.

Or: [85]

Remember, Lord, your compassion and mercy
     which you showed long ago.
Do not recall the sins and failings of my youth.
In your mercy remember me, Lord,
     because of your goodness.   (Psalm 25:6-7)

Or: [86]

Wash me from my guilt
and cleanse me of my sin.
I acknowledge my offense;
my sin is before me always. (Psalm 51:4-5)

Or: [87]

Father, I have sinned against you;
I no longer deserve to be called your son.
Be merciful to me, a sinner. (Luke 15:18; 18:13)

Or: [88]

Father of mercy,
like the prodigal son
I return to you and say:
"I have sinned against you
and am no longer worthy to be called your son."
Christ Jesus, Savior of the world,
I pray with the repentant thief
to whom you promised Paradise:
"Lord, remember me in your kingdom."
Holy Spirit, fountain of love,
I call on you with trust:
"Purify my heart,
and help me to walk as a child of light."

Or: [89]

Lord Jesus,
you opened the eyes of the blind,
healed the sick,
forgave the sinful woman,
and after Peter's denial confirmed him in your love.
Listen to my prayer:
forgive all my sins,
renew your love in my heart,
help me to live in perfect unity with my fellow Christians
that I may proclaim your saving power to all the world.

Or: [90]

Lord Jesus,
you chose to be called the friend of sinners.
By your saving death and resurrection

23

free me from my sins.
May your peace take root in my heart
and bring forth a harvest
of love, holiness, and truth.

Or: [91]

Lord Jesus Christ,
you are the Lamb of God;
you take away the sins of the world.
Through the grace of the Holy Spirit
restore me to friendship with your Father,
cleanse me from every stain of sin
in the blood you shed for me,
and raise me to new life
for the glory of your name.

Or: [92]

Lord God,
in your goodness have mercy on me:
do not look on my sins,
but take away all my guilt.
Create in me a clean heart
and renew within me an upright spirit.

Or:

Lord Jesus, Son of God,
have mercy on me, a sinner.

ABSOLUTION

46.   Then the priest extends his hands over the penitent's head (or at
least extends his right hand) and says:

God, the Father of mercies,
through the death and resurrection of his Son
has reconciled the world to himself
and sent the Holy Spirit among us
for the forgiveness of sins;
through the ministry of the Church
may God give you pardon and peace,
and **I absolve you from your sins
in the name of the Father, and of the Son, ✠
and of the Holy Spirit.**

℞.   Amen.

47.   After the absolution, the priest continues:

Give thanks to the Lord, for he is good.

℟.   **His mercy endures for ever.**

Then the priest dismisses the penitent who has been reconciled, saying:

The Lord has freed you from your sins. Go in peace.

Or: [93]

May the Passion of our Lord Jesus Christ,
the intercession of the Blessed Virgin Mary
  and of all the saints,
whatever good you do and suffering you endure,
heal your sins,
help you to grow in holiness,
and reward you with eternal life.
Go in peace.

Or:

The Lord has freed you from sin.
May he bring you safely to his kingdom in heaven.
Glory to him for ever.

℟.   **Amen.**

Or:

Blessed are those
whose sins have been forgiven,
whose evil deeds have been forgotten.
Rejoice in the Lord,
and go in peace.

Or:

Go in peace,
and proclaim to the world
the wonderful works of God,
who has brought you salvation.

CHAPTER II

RITE FOR RECONCILIATION OF SEVERAL PENITENTS WITH INDIVIDUAL CONFESSION AND ABSOLUTION

INTRODUCTORY RITES

Song

48.　When the faithful have assembled, they may sing a psalm, antiphon, or other appropriate song while the priest is entering the church, for example:

Hear us, Lord,
for you are merciful and kind.
In your great compassion,
look on us with love.

Or:

Let us come with confidence before the throne of grace
to receive God's mercy,
and we shall find pardon and strength
in our time of need.

Greeting

49.　After the song the priest greets the congregation:

Grace, mercy, and peace be with you
from God the Father
and Christ Jesus our Savior.

℞.　**And also with you.**

Or:

Grace and peace be with you
from God the Father

and from Jesus Christ
who loved us
and washed away our sins in his blood.

℟.   Glory to him for ever. Amen.

Or: [94]

Grace, mercy, and peace
from God the Father and Jesus Christ his Son
be with you in truth and love.

℟.   Amen.

Or: [95]

May God open your hearts to his law
and give you peace;
may he answer your prayers
and restore you to friendship.

℟.   Amen.

Or: [96]

Grace and peace be with you
from God our Father
and from the Lord Jesus Christ
who laid down his life for our sins.

℟.   Glory to him for ever. Amen.

Then the priest or another minister speaks briefly about the importance
and purpose of the celebration and the order of the service.

Opening Prayer

50.   The priest invites all to pray, using these or similar words:

**Brothers and sisters, God calls us to conversion; let us there-
fore ask him for the grace of sincere repentance.**

All pray in silence for a brief period. Then the priest sings or says the
prayer:

**Lord,
hear the prayers of those who call on you,
forgive the sins of those who confess to you,
and in your merciful love
give us your pardon and your peace.**

We ask this through Christ our Lord.

℟.   Amen.

Or:

Lord,
send your Spirit among us
to cleanse us in the waters of repentance.
May he make of us a living sacrifice
so that in every place,
by his life-giving power,
we may praise your glory
and proclaim your loving compassion.

We ask this through Christ our Lord.

℟.   Amen.

Or: [97]

Lord,
turn to us in mercy
and forgive us all our sins
that we may serve you in true freedom.

We ask this through Christ our Lord.

℟.   Amen.

Or: [98]

Lord our God,
you are patient with sinners
and accept our desire to make amends.
We acknowledge our sins
and are resolved to change our lives.
Help us to celebrate this sacrament of your mercy
so that we may reform our lives
and receive from you the gift of everlasting joy.

We ask this through Christ our Lord.

℟.   Amen.

Or: [99]

Almighty and merciful God,
you have brought us together in the name of your Son

29

to receive your mercy and grace in our time of need.
Open our eyes to see the evil we have done.
Touch our hearts and convert us to yourself.
Where sin has divided and scattered,
may your love make one again;
where sin has brought weakness,
may your power heal and strengthen;
where sin has brought death,
may your Spirit raise to new life.

Give us a new heart to love you,
so that our lives may reflect the image of your Son.
May the world see the glory of Christ
revealed in your Church,
and come to know
that he is the one whom you have sent,
Jesus Christ, your Son, our Lord.

℞. Amen.

Or: [100]

Father of mercies
and God of all consolation,
you do not wish the sinner to die
but to be converted and live.
Come to the aid of your people,
that they may turn from their sins
and live for you alone.
May we be attentive to your word,
confess our sins, receive your forgiveness,
and be always grateful for your loving kindness.
Help us to live the truth in love
and grow into the fullness of Christ, your Son,
who lives and reigns for ever and ever.

℞. Amen.

CELEBRATION OF THE WORD OF GOD

Reading the Word of God

51. The celebration of the word follows. If there are several readings a
psalm or other appropriate song or even a period of silence should inter-
vene between them, so that everyone may understand the word of God
more deeply and give it his heartfelt assent. If there is only one reading,
it is preferable that it be from the gospel.

30

Love is the fullness of the law

First Reading: Deuteronomy 5:1-3, 6-7, 11-12, 16-21a; 6:4-6

Love the Lord your God with all your heart.

Responsorial Psalm: Baruch 1:15-22

℞. (3:2) **Listen and have pity, Lord, because you are merciful.**

Second Reading: Ephesians 5:1-14

Walk in love, as Christ loved us.

Gospel Acclamation: John 8:12

**I am the light of the world.
The man who follows me will have the light of life.**

Gospel: Matthew 22:34-40

**On these two commandments
the whole law and the prophets depend.**

or: John 13:34-35; 15:10-13

**I give you a new commandment:
love one another.**

Second Example
Your mind must be renewed

First Reading: Isaiah 1:10-18

Stop doing what is wrong, and learn to do good.

Responsorial Psalm: Psalm 51, especially verses 18-19

℞. (19a) **A humbled heart is pleasing to God.**

Second Reading: Ephesians 4:23-32

Your mind must be renewed by a spiritual revolution.

Gospel Acclamation: Matthew 11:28

**Come to me, all you that labor and are burdened,
and I will give you rest.**

Gospel: Matthew 5:1-12

Happy the poor in spirit.

Other optional texts are given in nos. 101-201.

Homily

52.   The homily which follows is based on the texts of the readings and should lead the penitents to examine their consciences and renew their lives.

Examination of Conscience

53. A period of time may be spent in making an examination of conscience and in arousing true sorrow for sins. The priest, deacon, or another minister may help the faithful by brief statements or a kind of litany, taking into consideration their circumstances, age, etc.

RITE OF RECONCILIATION

General Confession of Sins

54. The deacon or another minister invites all to kneel or bow, and to join in saying a general formula for confession (for example, *I confess to almighty God*). Then they stand and say a litany or sing an appropriate song. The Lord's Prayer is always added at the end.

First Example

Deacon or minister:

My brothers and sisters, confess your sins and pray for each other, that you may be healed.

All say:

**I confess to almighty God,
and to you, my brothers and sisters,
that I have sinned through my own fault**

They strike their breast:

**in my thoughts and in my words,
in what I have done,
and in what I have failed to do;
and I ask blessed Mary, ever virgin,
all the angels and saints,
and you, my brothers and sisters,
to pray for me to the Lord our God.**

Deacon or minister:

The Lord is merciful. He makes us clean of heart and leads us out into his freedom when we acknowledge our guilt. Let us ask him to forgive us and bind up the wounds inflicted by our sins.

Give us the grace of true repentance.

℟. **We pray you, hear us.**

Pardon your servants and release them from the debt of sin.

℟. **We pray you, hear us.**

32

Forgive your children who confess their sins, and restore them to full communion with your Church.

℟.   We pray you, hear us.

Renew the glory of baptism in those who have lost it by sin.

℟.   We pray you, hear us.

Welcome them to your altar, and renew their spirit with the hope of eternal glory.

℟.   We pray you, hear us.

Keep them faithful to your sacraments and loyal in your service.

℟.   We pray you, hear us.

Renew your love in their hearts, and make them bear witness to it in their daily lives.

℟.   We pray you, hear us.

Keep them always obedient to your commandments and protect within them your gift of eternal life.

℟.   We pray you, hear us.

Deacon or minister:

Let us now pray to God our Father in the words Christ gave us, and ask him for his forgiveness and protection from all evil.

All say together:

Our Father . . .

The priest concludes:

Lord,
draw near to your servants
who in the presence of your Church
confess that they are sinners.
Through the ministry of the Church
free them from all sin
so that renewed in spirit
they may give you thankful praise.

We ask this through Christ our Lord.

℟.   Amen.

Deacon or minister:

> Brothers and sisters, let us call to mind the goodness of God our Father, and acknowledge our sins, so that we may receive his merciful forgiveness.

All say:

> I confess to almighty God,
> and to you, my brothers and sisters,
> that I have sinned through my own fault

They strike their breast:

> in my thoughts and in my words,
> in what I have done,
> and in what I have failed to do;
> and I ask blessed Mary, ever virgin,
> all the angels and saints,
> and you, my brothers and sisters,
> to pray for me to the Lord our God.

Deacon or minister:

> Christ our Savior is our advocate with the Father:
> with humble hearts let us ask him to forgive us our sins
> and cleanse us from every stain.
>
> You were sent with good news for the poor and healing for the contrite.

℟. Lord, be merciful to me, a sinner.

    Or:

    Lord, have mercy.

> You came to call sinners, not the just.

℟. Lord, be merciful to me, a sinner.

    Or:

    Lord, have mercy.

> You forgave the many sins of the woman who showed you great love.

℟. Lord, be merciful to me, a sinner.

Or:

Lord, have mercy.

You did not shun the company of outcasts and sinners.

℞. **Lord, be merciful to me, a sinner.**
   Or:

Lord, have mercy.

You carried back to the fold the sheep that had strayed.

℞. **Lord, be merciful to me, a sinner.**
   Or:

Lord, have mercy.

You did not condemn the woman taken in adultery, but sent her away in peace.

℞. **Lord, be merciful to me, a sinner.**
   Or:

Lord, have mercy.

You called Zacchaeus to repentance and a new life.

℞. **Lord, be merciful to me, a sinner.**
   Or:

Lord, have mercy.

You promised Paradise to the repentant thief.

℞. **Lord, be merciful to me, a sinner.**
   Or:

Lord, have mercy.

You are always interceding for us at the right hand of the Father.

℞. **Lord, be merciful to me, a sinner.**
   Or:

Lord, have mercy.

Deacon or minister:

Now, in obedience to Christ himself, let us join in prayer to the Father, asking him to forgive us as we forgive others.

All say together:

Our Father . . .

The priest concludes:

Father, our source of life,
you know our weakness.
May we reach out with joy to grasp your hand
and walk more readily in your ways.

We ask this through Christ our Lord.

℟.   **Amen.**

ALTERNATE EXAMPLES FOR GENERAL CONFESSION OF SINS.

PRAYER DIRECTED TO THE FATHER

Invitation   [202]

Dear friends in Christ, our merciful Father does not desire the death of the sinner but rather that he should turn back to him and have life. Let us pray that we who are sorry for our past sins may fear no future evil and sin no more.

℟.   **Spare us, Lord; spare your people.**

Or:

God who is infinitely merciful pardons all who are repentant and takes away their guilt. Confident in his goodness, let us ask him to forgive all our sins as we confess them with sincerity of heart.

℟.   **Lord, hear our prayer.**

Or:

God gave us his Son for our sins and raised him up to make us holy. Let us humbly pray to the Father.

℟.   **Lord, have mercy on your people.**

Or:

God our Father waits for the return of those who are lost and welcomes them back as his children. Let us pray that we may turn back to him and be received with kindness into his house.

℟.   **Lord, do not hold our sins against us.**

Or:

℞. Father, we have sinned in your sight; we are unworthy to be called your children.

Or:

Our God seeks out what is lost, leads home the abandoned, binds up what is broken and gives strength to the weak; let us ask him to help us.

℞. Lord, heal our weakness.

Intercessions

(At least one of the intercessions should always be a petition for a true conversion of heart.)

[204]

By human weakness we have disfigured the holiness of the Church: pardon all our sins and restore us to full communion with our brethren.

℞. Lord, hear our prayer.   Or: Lord, hear us.

(Or another suitable response may be used.)

Your mercy is our hope: welcome us to the sacrament of reconciliation. ℞.

Give us the will to change our lives, and the lives of others, by charity, good example and prayer. ℞.

As we make our confession, rescue us from slavery to sin and lead us to the freedom enjoyed by your children. ℞.

Make us a living sign of your love for all to see: people reconciled with you and with each other. ℞

Through the sacrament of reconciliation may we grow in your peace and seek to spread it throughout the world. ℞.

In this sign of your love you forgive us our sins: may it teach us to love others and to forgive their sins against us. ℞.

In your mercy clothe us in the wedding garment of grace and welcome us to your table. ℞.

Forgive us our sins, lead us in the ways of goodness and love, and bring us to the reward of everlasting peace. ℞.

Give light to our darkness and lead us by your truth.   ℟.

In justice you punish us: in your mercy set us free for the glory of your name.   ℟.

May your power keep safe from all danger those whom your love sets free from the chains of sin.   ℟.

Look on our weakness: do not be angry and condemn, but in your love cleanse, guide and save us.   ℟.

In your mercy free us from the past and enable us to begin a new life of holiness.   ℟.

When we stray from you, guide us back into the way of holiness, love and peace.   ℟.

By your redeeming love overcome our sinfulness and the harm it has brought us.   ℟.

Blot out the sins of the past and fit us for the life that is to come.   ℟.

Or:

The following intercessions may be used with a variable response or with an invariable response as in the Liturgy of the Hours.

In your goodness forgive our sins against the unity of your family,
—make us one in heart, one in spirit.

We have sinned, Lord, we have sinned,
—take away our sins by your saving grace.

Give us pardon for our sins,
—and reconciliation with your Church.

Touch our hearts and change our lives, make us grow always in your friendship,
—help us to make up for our sins against your wisdom and goodness.

Cleanse and renew your Church, Lord,
—may it grow in strength as a witness to you.

Touch the hearts of those who have abandoned you through sin and scandal,
—call them back to you and keep them faithful in your love.

May we show forth in our lives the sufferings of your Son,
—you raised us up to life when you raised him from the dead.

Have mercy on us, Lord, as we praise and thank you,
—with your pardon give us also your peace.

Lord, our sins are many, but we trust in your mercy,
—call us, and we shall turn to you.

Receive us as we come before you with humble and contrite hearts,
—those who trust in you shall never trust in vain.

We have turned away from you and fallen into sin,
—we have followed evil ways and rejected your commandments.

Turn to us, Lord, and show us your mercy; blot out our sins,
—cast them into the depths of the sea.

Restore us, Lord, to your favor, and give us joy in your presence,
—may our glory be to serve you with all our hearts.

PRAYER DIRECTED TO CHRIST

Invitation [203]

Jesus Christ is the victor over life and death: in his mercy may he pardon our offenses against God and reconcile us with the Church we have wounded by our sins.

℟. Lord Jesus, be our salvation.

Or:

In his great love Christ willingly suffered and died for our sins and for the sins of all mankind. Let us come before him with faith and hope to pray for the salvation of the world.

℟. Christ, graciously hear us.

Or:

Let us pray with confidence to Christ, the Good Shepherd, who seeks out the lost sheep and carries it back with joy.

℟. Lord, seek us out and bring us home.

Or:

Christ our Lord bore our sins upon the cross and by his suffering has brought us healing, so that we live for God and are dead to sin. Let us pray with humility and trust.

℟. Lord, to whom shall we go? You have the words of eternal life. We have come to believe and to know that you are the Christ, the Son of God.

Or:

℟. Have pity on us, and help us.

Or:

Christ our Lord was given up to death for our sins and rose again for our justification. Let us pray to him with confidence in his goodness.

℟. You are our Savior.

Or:

℟. Jesus Christ, Son of the living God, have pity on us.

Intercessions: [205]

By your death you reconciled us with the Father and brought us salvation.

(Romans 5:10)

℟. Lord, have mercy.   Or: Christ, hear us.

(Or another suitable response may be used.)

You died and rose again, and sit at the right hand of the Father, to make intercession for us. ℟.

(Romans 8:34)

You came from God as our wisdom and justice, our sanctification and redemption. ℟.

(1 Corinthians 1:30)

You washed mankind in the Spirit of our God; you made us holy and righteous. ℟.

(1 Corinthians 6:11)

You warned us that if we sin against each other we sin against you. ℟.

(1 Corinthians 8:12)

Though you were rich you became poor for our sake, so that by your poverty we might become rich. ℟.

(2 Corinthians 8:9)

You gave yourself up for our sins to save us from this evil world. ℟.

(Galatians 1:4)

You rose from the dead to save us from the anger that was to come. ℟.

(1 Thessalonians 1:10)

You came into the world to save sinners. ℟.

(1 Timothy 1:15)

You gave yourself up to bring redemption to all. ℟.

(1 Timothy 2:6)

You destroyed death and gave light to life. ℟.

(2 Timothy 1:10)

You will come to judge the living and the dead. ℟.

(2 Timothy 4:1)

You gave yourself up for us to redeem us from all sin and to prepare for yourself a holy people, marked as your own, devoted to good works. ℟.

(Titus 2:14)

You showed us your mercy, and as a faithful high priest in the things of God you made atonement for the sins of the people. ℟.

(Hebrews 2:17)

You became the source of salvation for all who obey you. ℟.

(Hebrews 5:9)

Through the Holy Spirit you offered yourself to God as a spotless victim, cleansing our consciences from lifeless works. ℟.

(Hebrews 9:15)

You were offered in sacrifice to undo the sins of the many. ℟.

(Hebrews 9:28)

Once and for all you died for our sins, the innocent one for the guilty. ℟.

(1 Peter 3:18)

You are the atonement for our sins and for the sins of the world. ℟.

(1 John 2:2)

You died that those who believe in you may not perish but have eternal life. ℟.

(John 3:16, 35)

You came into the world to seek and save what was lost. ℟.

(Matthew 18:11)

You were sent, by the Father, not to judge the world but to save it. ℟.   (John 3:17)

You have power on earth to forgive sins. ℟.   (Mark 2:10)

You invite all who labor and are burdened to come to you to be refreshed. ℟.   (Matthew 11:28)

You gave your apostles the keys of the kingdom of heaven, the power to bind and to loose. ℟.   (Matthew 16:19; 18:18)

You told us that the whole law depends on love of God and of our neighbor. ℟.   (Matthew 22:38-40)

Jesus, life of all mankind, you came into the world to give us life, life in its fullness. ℟.   (John 10:10)

Jesus, Good Shepherd, you gave your life for your sheep. ℟.
(John 10:11)

Jesus, eternal truth, you give us true freedom. ℟.
(John 14:6; 8:32, 36)

Jesus, you are the way to the Father. ℟.   (John 14:6)

Jesus, you are the resurrection and life; those who believe in you, even if they are dead, will live. ℟.

(John 11:25)

Jesus, true vine, the Father prunes your branches to make them bear even greater fruit. ℟.   (John 15:1-2)

Or:

The following intercessions may be used with a variable response or with an invariable response as in the Liturgy of the Hours.

Healer of body and soul, bind up the wounds of our hearts,
—that our lives may grow strong through grace.

Help us to strip ourselves of sin,
—and put on the new life of grace.

Redeemer of the world, give us the spirit of penance and a deeper devotion to your passion,
—so that we may have a fuller share in your risen glory.

May your Mother, the refuge of sinners, intercede for us,
—and ask you in your goodness to pardon our sins.

You forgave the woman who repented,
—show us also your mercy.

You brought back the lost sheep on your shoulders,
—pity us and lead us home.

You promised paradise to the good thief,
—take us with you into your Kingdom.

You died for us and rose again,
—make us share in your death and resurrection.

Individual Confession and Absolution

55.   Then the penitents go to the priests designated for individual confession, and confess their sins. Each one receives and accepts a fitting
act of satisfaction and is absolved. After hearing the confession and
offering suitable counsel, the priest extends his hands over the penitent's
head (or at least extends his right hand) and gives him absolution. Everything else which is customary in individual confession is omitted.

God, the Father of mercies,
through the death and resurrection of his Son
has reconciled the world to himself
and sent the Holy Spirit among us
for the forgiveness of sins;
through the ministry of the Church
may God give you pardon and peace,
and I absolve you from your sins
in the name of the Father, and of the Son, ✠
and of the Holy Spirit.

℟.   **Amen.**

PROCLAMATION OF PRAISE

Proclamation of Praise for God's Mercy

56.   When the individual confessions have been completed, the other
priests stand near the one who is presiding over the celebration. The latter
invites all present to offer thanks and encourages them to do good works
which will proclaim the grace of repentance in the life of the entire community and each of its members. It is fitting for all to sing a psalm or
hymn or to say a litany in acknowledgment of God's power and mercy,
for example, the canticle of Mary (Luke 1:46-55), or Psalm 136:1-9,
13-14, 16, 25-26.

Or one of the following: [206]

Psalm 32:1-7, 10-11
℟.   **Rejoice in the Lord and sing for joy, friends of God.**

Psalm 98:1-9
℟.   **The Lord has remembered his mercy.**

Psalm 100:2-5
℟.   **The Lord is loving and kind: his mercy is for ever.**

Psalm 119:1, 10-13, 15-16, 18, 33, 105, 169, 170, 174-175
℟. **Blessed are you, Lord; teach me your decrees.**

Psalm 103:1-4, 8-18
℟. **The mercy of the Lord is from everlasting to everlasting on those who revere him.**

Psalm 145:1-21
℟. **Day after day I will bless you, Lord: I will praise your name for ever.**

Psalm 146:2-10
℟. **I will sing to my God all the days of my life.**

Isaiah 12:1b-6
℟. **Praise the Lord and call upon his name.**

Isaiah 61:10-11
℟. **My spirit rejoices in my God.**

Jeremiah 31:10-14
℟. **The Lord has redeemed his people.**

Daniel 3:52-57
℟. **Bless the Lord, all the works of his hand: praise and glorify him for ever.**

Luke 1:46-55
℟. **The Lord has remembered his mercy.**

Ephesians 1:3-10
℟. **Blessed be God who chose us in Christ.**

Revelation 15:3-4
℟. **Great and wonderful are all your works, Lord.**

Concluding Prayer of Thanksgiving

57. After the song of praise or the litany, the priest concludes the common prayer:

**Almighty and merciful God,
how wonderfully you created man
and still more wonderfully remade him.
You do not abandon the sinner
but seek him out with a father's love.
You sent your Son into the world
to destroy sin and death
by his passion
and to restore life and joy
by his passion,**

44

You sent the Holy Spirit into our hearts
to make us your children
and heirs of your kingdom.
You constantly renew our spirit
in the sacraments of your redeeming love,
freeing us from slavery to sin
and transforming us ever more closely
into the likeness of your beloved Son.
We thank you for the wonders of your mercy,
and with heart and hand and voice
we join with the whole Church
in a new song of praise:
Glory to you
through Christ
in the Holy Spirit,
now and for ever.

℞.   Amen.

Or:

All-holy Father,
you have shown us your mercy
and made us a new creation
in the likeness of your Son.
Make us living signs of your love
for the whole world to see.

We ask this through Christ our Lord.

℞.   Amen.

Or: [207]

Father, all-powerful and ever-living God,
we do well always and everywhere to give you thanks.

When you punish us, you show your justice;
when you pardon us, you show your kindness;
yet always your mercy enfolds us.

When you chastise us, you do not wish to condemn us;
when you spare us, you give us time to make amends for our sins
through Christ our Lord.

℞.   Amen.

Or: [208]

Lord God,
creator and ruler of your kingdom of light,
in your great love for this world
you gave up your only Son
for our salvation.
His cross has redeemed us,
his death has given us life,
his resurrection has raised us to glory.
Through him we ask you
to be always present among your family.
Teach us to be reverent in the presence of your glory;
fill our hearts with faith,
our days with good works,
our lives with your love;
may your truth be on our lips
and your wisdom in all our actions,
that we may receive the reward of everlasting life.

We ask this through Christ our Lord.

℟. Amen.

Or: [209]

Lord Jesus Christ,
your loving forgiveness knows no limits.
You took our human nature
to give us an example of humility
and to make us faithful in every trial.
May we never lose the gifts you have given us,
but if we fall into sin,
lift us up by your gift of repentance,
for you live and reign for ever and ever.

℟. Amen.

Or: [210]

Father,
in your love you have brought us
from evil to good and from misery to happiness.
Through your blessings
give the courage of perseverance
to those you have called and justified by faith.

46

Grant this through Christ our Lord.

℟. Amen.

Or: [211]

God and Father of us all,
you have forgiven our sins
and sent us your peace.
Help us to forgive each other
and to work together to establish peace in the world.

We ask this through Christ our Lord.

℟. Amen.

CONCLUDING RITE

Blessing

58. Then the priest blesses all present:

May the Lord guide your hearts in the way of his love
and fill you with Christ-like patience.

℟. Amen.

May he give you strength
to walk in newness of life
and to please him in all things.

℟. Amen.

May almighty God bless you,
The Father, and the Son, ✠ and the Holy Spirit.

℟. Amen.

Or: [212]

And may the blessing of almighty God,
the Father, and the Son, ✠ and the Holy Spirit,
come upon you and remain with you for ever.

℟. Amen.

Or: [213]

May the Father bless us,
for we are his children, born to eternal life.

℟. Amen.

May the Son show us his saving power,
for he died and rose for us.

℞. Amen.

May the Spirit give us his gift of holiness
and lead us by the right path,
for he dwells in our hearts.

℞. Amen.

Or: [214]

May the Father bless us,
for he has adopted us as his children.

℞. Amen.

May the Son come to help us,
for he has received us as brothers and sisters.

℞. Amen.

May the Spirit be with us,
for he has made us his dwelling place.

℞. Amen.

DISMISSAL

59.   The deacon or other minister or the priest himself dismisses the
assembly:

The Lord has freed you from your sins. Go in peace.

All answer:

Thanks to be God.

(Any other appropriate form may be used.)

48

CHAPTER III
RITE FOR RECONCILIATION
OF SEVERAL PENITENTS WITH
CONFESSION AND ABSOLUTION

60.   For the reconciliation of several penitents with general confession and absolution, in the cases provided for in the law, everything is done as described above for the reconciliation of several penitents with individual absolution, but with the following changes only.

INSTRUCTION

After the homily or as part of the homily, the priest explains to the faithful who wish to receive general absolution that they should be properly disposed. Each one should repent of his sins and resolve to turn away from these sins, to make up for any scandal and harm he may have caused, and to confess individually at the proper time each of the serious sins which cannot now be confessed. Some form of satisfaction should be proposed to all, and each individual may add something if he desires.

GENERAL CONFESSION

61.   Then the deacon or other minister or the priest himself invites the penitents who wish to receive absolution to indicate this by some kind of sign. He may say:

Will those of you who wish to receive sacramental absolution please kneel and acknowledge that you are sinners.

Or:

Will those of you who wish to receive sacramental absolution please bow your heads and acknowledge that you are sinners.

Or he may suggest a sign laid down by the episcopal conference.

The penitents say a general formula for confession (for example, *I confess to almighty God*). A litany or appropriate song may follow, as described above for the reconciliation of several penitents with individual confession and absolution (no. 54). The Lord's Prayer is always added at the end.

GENERAL ABSOLUTION

62. The priest then gives absolution, holding his hands extended over the penitents and saying:

**God the Father does not wish the sinner to die
but to turn back to him and live.
He loved us first and sent his Son into the world to be its Savior.
May he show you his merciful love and give you peace.**

℞. **Amen.**

**Our Lord Jesus Christ was given up to death for our sins,
and rose again for our justification.
He sent the Holy Spirit on his apostles
and gave them power to forgive sins.
Through the ministry entrusted to me
may he deliver you from evil
and fill you with his Holy Spirit.**

℞. **Amen.**

**The Spirit, the Comforter, was given to us for the forgiveness
of sins.
In him we approach the Father.
May he cleanse your hearts and clothe you in his glory,
so that you may proclaim the mighty acts of God
who has called you out of darkness into the splendor of
his light.**

℞. **Amen.**

And **I absolve you from your sins
in the name of the Father, and of the Son, ✠
and of the Holy Spirit.**

℞. **Amen.**

Or:

> **God, the Father of mercies,**
> **through the death and resurrection of his Son**
> **has reconciled the world to himself**
> **and sent the Holy Spirit among us**
> **for the forgiveness of sins;**
> **through the ministry of the Church**
> **may God give you pardon and peace,**
> **and I absolve you from your sins**
> **in the name of the Father, and of the Son, ✠**
> **and of the Holy Spirit.**
>
> ℟. **Amen.**

Proclamation of Praise and Conclusion

63.   The priest invites all to thank God and to acknowledge his mercy. After a suitable song or hymn, he blesses the people and dismisses them, as described above, nos. 58-59, but without the concluding prayer (no. 57).

SHORT RITE

64.   In case of necessity, the rite for reconciling several penitents with general confession and absolution may be shortened. If possible, there is a brief reading from scripture. After giving the usual instruction (no. 60) and indicating the act of penance, the priest invites the penitents to make a general confession (for example, *I confess to almighty God*), and gives the absolution with the form which is indicated in no. 62.

65.   In imminent danger of death, it is enough for the priest to use the form of absolution itself. In this case it may be shortened to the following:

> **I absolve you from your sins**
> **in the name of the Father, and of the Son, ✠**
> **and of the Holy Spirit.**
>
> ℟. **Amen.**

66.   A person who receives general absolution from grave sins is bound to confess each grave sin at his next individual confession.

CHAPTER IV
VARIOUS TEXTS USED IN THE CELEBRATION OF RECONCILIATION

I. FOR THE RECONCILIATION OF ONE PENITENT

INVITATION TO TRUST IN GOD

67. Ezekiel 33:11

    The Lord does not wish the sinner to die
    but to turn back to him and live.
    Come before him with trust in his mercy.

68. Luke 5:32

    May the Lord Jesus welcome you.
    He came to call sinners, not the just.
    Have confidence in him.

69.

    May the grace of the Holy Spirit
    fill your heart with light,
    that you may confess your sins with loving trust
    and come to know that God is merciful.

70.

    May the Lord be in your heart
    and help you to confess your sins with true sorrow.

71. 1 John 2:1-2

    If you have sinned, do not lose heart.
    We have Jesus Christ to plead for us with the Father:
    he is the holy One,
    the atonement for our sins
    and for the sins of the whole world.

SHORT READINGS FROM SCRIPTURE

72.

    Let us look on Jesus
    who suffered to save us
    and rose again for our justification.

53

Isaiah 53:4-6

**Yet it was our infirmities that he bore,
our sufferings that he endured,
While we thought of him as stricken,
as one smitten by God and afflicted.
But he was pierced for our offenses,
crushed for our sins,
Upon him was the chastisement that
makes us whole,
by his stripes we were healed.
We had all gone astray like sheep,
each following his own way;
But the Lord laid upon him
the guilt of us all.**

73.   Ezekiel 11:19-20

Let us listen to the Lord as he speaks to us:

I will give them a new heart and put a new spirit within them; I will remove the stony heart from their bodies, and replace it with a natural heart, so that they will live according to my statutes, and observe and carry out my ordinances; thus they shall be my people and I will be their God.

74.   Matthew 6:14-15

Let us listen to the Lord as he speaks to us:

If you forgive the faults of others, your heavenly Father will forgive you yours. If you do not forgive others, neither will your Father forgive you.

75.   Mark 1:14-15

After John's arrest, Jesus appeared in Galilee proclaiming the good news of God: "This is the time of fulfillment. The reign of God is at hand! Reform your lives and believe in the gospel!"

76.   Luke 6:31-38

Let us listen to the Lord as he speaks to us:

Do to others what you would have them do to you. If you love those who love you, what credit is that to you? Even sinners love those who love them. If you do good to those who do good to you, how can you claim any credit? Sinners do as much. If you lend to those from whom you expect repayment, what merit is there in it for you? Even sinners lend to sinners, expecting to be repaid in full.

Love your enemy and do good; lend without expecting repayment. Then will your recompense be great. You will rightly be called sons of the Most High, since he himself is good to the ungrateful and the wicked.

"Be compassionate, as your Father is compassionate. Do not judge, and you will not be judged. Do not condemn, and you will not be condemned. Pardon, and you shall be pardoned. Give, and it shall be given to you. Good measure pressed down, shaken together, running over, will they pour into the fold of your garment. For the measure you measure with will be measured back to you."

77.   Luke 15:1-7

The tax collectors and sinners were all gathering around to hear him, at which the Pharisees and the scribes murmured, "This man welcomes sinners and eats with them." Then he addressed this parable to them: "Who among you, if he has a hundred sheep and loses one of them, does not leave the ninety-nine in the wasteland and follow the lost one until he finds it? And when he finds it, he puts it on his shoulders in jubilation. Once arrived home, he invites friends and neighbors in and says to them, 'Rejoice with me because I have found my lost sheep.' I tell you, there will likewise be more joy in heaven over one repentant sinner than over ninety-nine righteous people who have no need to repent.

78.   John 20:19-23

On the evening of that first day of the week, even though the disciples had locked the doors of the place where they were for fear of the Jews, Jesus came and stood before them. "Peace be with you," he said. When he had said this, he showed them his hands and his side. At the sight of the Lord the disciples rejoiced. "Peace be with you," he said again.

"As the Father has sent me,
so I send you."

Then he breathed on them and said:

"Receive the Holy Spirit.
If you forgive men's sins,
they are forgiven them;
if you hold them bound,
they are held bound."

79. Romans 5:8-9

It is precisely in this that God proves his love for us: that while we were still sinners, Christ died for us. Now that we have been justified by his blood, it is all the more certain that we shall be saved by him from God's wrath.

80. Ephesians 5:1-2

Be imitators of God as his dear children. Follow the way of love, even as Christ loved you. He gave himself for us as an offering to God, a gift of pleasing fragrance.

81. Colossians 1:12-14

Give thanks to the Father for having made you worthy to share the lot of the saints in light. He rescued us from the power of darkness and brought us into the kingdom of his beloved Son. Through him we have redemption, the forgiveness of our sins.

82. Colossians 3:8-10, 12-17

You must put that aside now: all the anger and quick temper, the malice, the insults, the foul language. Stop lying to one another. What you have done is put aside your old self with its past deeds and put on a new man, one who grows in knowledge as he is formed anew in the image of his Creator.

Because you are God's chosen ones, holy and beloved, clothe yourselves with heartfelt mercy, with kindness, humility, meekness, and patience. Bear with one another; forgive whatever grievances you have against one another. Forgive as the Lord has forgiven you. Over all these virtues put on love, which binds the rest together and makes them perfect. Christ's peace must reign in your hearts, since as members of the one body you have been called to that peace. Dedicate yourselves to thankfulness. Let the word of Christ, rich as it is, dwell in you. In wisdom made perfect, instruct and admonish one another. Sing gratefully to God from your hearts in psalms, hymns, and inspired songs. Whatever you do, whether in speech or in action, do it in the name of Lord Jesus. Give thanks to God the Father through him.

83. 1 John 1:6-7, 9

If we say, "We have fellowship with him,"
while continuing to walk in darkness,
we are liars and do not act in truth.
But if we walk in light,

as he is in the light,
we have fellowship with one another,
and the blood of his Son Jesus cleanses us
from all sin.

But if we acknowledge our sins,
he who is just can be trusted
to forgive our sins
and cleanse us from every wrong.

84.   A reading may also be chosen from those given in nos. 101-201 for the reconciliation of several penitents. The priest and penitent may choose other readings from scripture.

PRAYER OF THE PENITENT

85.   Psalm 25:6-7

Remember, Lord, your compassion and mercy
    which you showed long ago.
Do not recall the sins and failings of my youth.
In your mercy remember me, Lord,
    because of your goodness.

86.   Psalm 51:4-5

Wash me from my guilt
and cleanse me of my sin.
I acknowledge my offense;
my sin is before me always.

87.   Luke 15:18, 18:13

Father, I have sinned against you;
I no longer deserve to be called your son.
Be merciful to me, a sinner.

88.

Father of mercy,
like the prodigal son
I return to you and say:
"I have sinned against you
and am no longer worthy to be called your son."
Christ Jesus, Savior of the world,
I pray with the repentant thief
to whom you promised paradise:
"Lord, remember me in your kingdom."
Holy Spirit, fountain of love,

I call on you with trust:
"Purify my heart,
and help me to walk as a child of the light."

89.

Lord Jesus,
you opened the eyes of the blind,
healed the sick,
forgave the sinful woman,
and after Peter's denial confirmed him in your love.
Listen to my prayer:
forgive all my sins,
renew your love in my heart,
help me to live in perfect unity with my fellow Christians
that I may proclaim your saving power to all the world.

90.

Lord Jesus,
you chose to be called the friend of sinners.
By your saving death and resurrection
free me from my sins.
May your peace take root in my heart
and bring forth a harvest
of love, holiness, and truth.

91.

Lord Jesus Christ,
you are the Lamb of God;
you take away the sins of the world.
Through the grace of the Holy Spirit
restore me to friendship with your Father,
cleanse me from every stain of sin
in the blood you shed for me,
and raise me to new life
for the glory of your name.

92.

Lord God,
in your goodness have mercy on me:
do not look on my sins,
but take away all my guilt.
Create in me a clean heart
and renew within me an upright spirit.

Or:

Lord Jesus, Son of God,
have mercy on me, a sinner.

93. In place of the proclamation of God's praise and the dismissal, the priest may say:

> May the Passion of our Lord Jesus Christ,
> the intercession of the Blessed Virgin Mary
>   and of all the saints,
> whatever good you do and suffering you endure,
> heal your sins,
> help you to grow in holiness,
> and reward you with eternal life.
> Go in peace.

Or:

> The Lord has freed you from sin.
> May he bring you safely to his kingdom in heaven.
> Glory to him for ever.

> ℟. Amen.

Or:

> Blessed are those
> whose sins have been forgiven,
> whose evil deeds have been forgotten.
> Rejoice in the Lord,
> and go in peace.

Or:

> Go in peace,
> and proclaim to the world
> the wonderful works of God,
> who has brought you salvation.

II. FOR THE RECONCILIATION OF SEVERAL PENITENTS

GREETING

94.

> Grace, mercy, and peace
> from God the Father and Jesus Christ his Son
> be with you in truth and love.

> ℟. Amen.

95.

May God open your hearts to his law
and give you peace;
may he answer your prayers
and restore you to his friendship.

℟. Amen.

96.

Grace and peace be with you
from God our Father
and from the Lord Jesus Christ
who laid down his life for our sins.

℟. Glory to him for ever. Amen.

The greetings from the introductory rites of Mass may also be used.

OPENING PRAYERS

97.

Lord,
turn to us in mercy
and forgive us all our sins
that we may serve you in true freedom.

We ask this through Christ our Lord.

℟. Amen.

98.

Lord our God,
you are patient with sinners
and accept our desire to make amends.
We acknowledge our sins
and are resolved to change our lives.
Help us to celebrate this sacrament of your mercy
so that we may reform our lives
and receive from you the gift of everlasting joy.

We ask this through Christ our Lord.

℟. Amen.

99.

Almighty and merciful God,
you have brought us together in the name of your Son
to receive your mercy and grace in our time of need.
Open our eyes to see the evil we have done.
Touch our hearts and convert us to yourself.

Where sin has divided and scattered,
may your love make one again;
where sin has brought weakness,
may your power heal and strengthen;
where sin has brought death,
may your Spirit raise to new life.

Give us a new heart to love you,
so that our lives may reflect the image of your Son.
May the world see the glory of Christ
revealed in your Church,
and come to know
that he is the one whom you have sent,
Jesus Christ, your Son, our Lord.

℞. Amen.

100.

Father of mercies
and God of all consolation,
you do not wish the sinner to die
but to be converted and live.
Come to the aid of your people,
that they may turn from their sins
and live for you alone.
May we be attentive to your word,
confess our sins, receive your forgiveness,
and be always grateful for your loving kindness.
Help us to live the truth in love
and grow into the fullness of Christ, your Son,
who lives and reigns for ever and ever.

℞. Amen.

BIBLICAL READINGS

The following readings are proposed as a help for pastors and others involved in the selection of readings. For diversity, and according to the nature of the group, other readings may be selected.

READINGS FROM THE OLD TESTAMENT

101. Genesis 3:1-19: She took the fruit of the tree and ate it.

102. Genesis 4:1-15: Cain set on his brother and killed him.

103. Genesis 18:17-33: The Lord said: I will not destroy the city for the sake of ten good men.

104. Exodus 17:1-7: They tempted the Lord saying: Is the Lord here or not?

105. Exodus 20:1-21: I am the Lord your God . . . you will not have other gods.

106. Deuteronomy 6:3-9: Love the Lord your God with your whole heart.

107. Deuteronomy 9:7-19: Your people quickly turned away from the wrong you had showed them.

108. Deuteronomy 30:15-20: I set before you life and prosperity, death and evil.

109. 2 Samuel 12:1-9, 13: David said to Nathan: I have sinned against the Lord God. Nathan said to David: The Lord has forgiven your sin; you will not die.

110. Nehemiah 9:1-20: The sons of Israel assembled for a fast and confessed their sins.

111. Wisdom: 1:1-16: Love justice, for wisdom will not enter an evil soul nor live in a body subjected to sin.

112. Wisdom 5:1-16: The hope of the wicked is like down flying on the wind. The just, however, live for ever.

113. Sirach 28:1-7: Forgive your neighbor when he hurts you, and then your sins will be forgiven when you pray.

114. Isaiah 1:2-6, 15-18: I have nourished and educated sons; however they have rebelled against me.

115. Isaiah 5:1-7: The vineyard became my delight. He looked for grapes, but it yielded wild grapes.

116. Isaiah 43:22-28: On account of me your iniquities are blotted out.

117. Isaiah 53:1-12: The Lord laid upon him our guilt.

118. Isaiah 55:1-11: Let the wicked man forsake his way and return to the Lord, and he will have mercy on him because he is generous in forgiving.

119. Isaiah 58:1-11: When you give your soul to the hungry and fulfill the troubled soul, your light will rise like dawn from the darkness, and your darkness will be like midday.

120. Isaiah 59:1-4, 9-15: Your iniquities divide you and your God.

121. Jeremiah 2:1-13: My people have done two evils: they have abandoned me, the fountain of living water, and have dug for themselves broken cisterns which hold no water.

122. Jeremiah 7:21-26: Listen to my voice, and I will be your God, and you will be my people.

123. Ezekiel 11:14-21: I will take the heart of stone from their bodies, and I will give them a heart of flesh, so that they may walk according to my laws.

124. Ezekiel 18:20-32: If a wicked man turns away from his sins, he shall live and not die.

125. Ezekiel 36:23-28: I shall sprinkle upon you clean water, put my spirit within you, and make you walk according to my commands.

126. Hosea 2:16-25: I will make a covenant for them on that day.

127. Hosea 11:1-11: I took them in my arms, and they did not know that I cured them.

128. Hosea 14:2-10: Israel, return to the Lord your God.

129. Joel 2:12-19: Return to me with your whole heart.

130. Micah 6:1-4, 6-8: Do right and love mercy, and walk humbly with your God.

131. Ezekiel 36:23-28: The Lord will turn back and have mercy on us; he will cast all our sins into the depths of the sea.

132. Zechariah 1:1-6: Return to me, and I shall return to you.

RESPONSORIAL PSALM

133. Psalm 13
℟. (6a) **All my hope, O Lord, is in your loving kindness.**

134. Psalm 25
℟. (16a) **Turn to me, Lord, and have mercy.**

135. Psalm 31:1-6
℟. (6b) **You have redeemed us, Lord, God of truth.**

136. Psalm 32
℟. (5c) **Lord, forgive the wrong I have done.**

137. Psalm 36
℟. (8) **How precious is your unfailing love, Lord.**

138. Psalm 50:7-8, 14-23
℟. (23b) **To the upright I will show the saving power of God.**

139. Psalm 51
℟. (14a) **Give back to me the joy of your salvation.**

140. Psalm 73
℟. (28a) **It is good for me to be with the Lord.**

141. Psalm 90
℟. (14) **Fill us with your love, O Lord, and we will sing for joy!**

142. Psalm 95
℟. (8a) **If today you hear his voice, harden not your hearts.**

143. Psalm 119:1, 10-13, 15-16
℟. (1) **Happy are they who follow the law of the Lord!**

144. Psalm 123
℟. (2c) **Our eyes are fixed on the Lord.**

145. Psalm 130
℟. (7bc) **With the Lord there is mercy, and fullness of redemption.**

146. Psalm 139:1-18, 23-24
℟. (23a) **You have searched me, and you know me, Lord.**

147. Psalm 143:1-11
℟. (10) **Teach me to do your will, my God.**

READINGS FROM THE NEW TESTAMENT

148. Romans 3:22-26: All men are justified by the gift of God through redemption in Christ Jesus.

149. Romans 5:6-11: We give glory to God through our Lord Jesus Christ, through whom we have received reconciliation.

150. Romans 6:2b-13: Consider yourselves dead to sin but alive to God.

151. Romans 6:16-23: The wages of sin is death; the gift of God is eternal life in Christ Jesus our Lord.

152. Romans 7:14-25: Unhappy man am I! Who will free me? Thanks to God through Jesus Christ our Lord.

153. Romans 12:1-2, 9-19: Be transformed by the renewal of your mind.

154. Romans 13:8-14: Let us cast away the works of darkness and put on the weapons of light.

155. 2 Corinthians 5:17-21: God reconciled the world to himself through Christ.

156. Galatians 5:16-24: You cannot belong to Christ unless you crucify the flesh with its passions and concupiscence.

157. Ephesians 2:1-10: When we were dead to sin, God, on account of his great love for us, brought us to life in Christ.

158. Ephesians 4:1-3, 17-32: Renew yourself and put on the new man.

159. Ephesians 5:1-14: You were once in darkness; now you are light in the Lord, so walk as children of light.

160. Ephesians 6:10-18: Put God's armor on so that you will be able to stand firm against evil.

161. Colossians 3:1-10, 12-17: If you were raised to life with Christ, aspire to the realm above. Put to death what remains in this earthly life.

162. Hebrews 12:1-5: You have not resisted to the point of shedding your blood in your struggle against sin.

163. James 1:22-27: Be doers of the word and not merely listeners.

164. James 2:14-26: What use is it if someone says that he believes and does not mainfest it in works?

165. James 3:1-12: If someone does not offend in word, he is a perfect man.

166. 1 Peter 1:13-23: You have been redeemed not by perishable goods, gold or silver, but by the precious blood of Jesus Christ.

167. 2 Peter 1:3-11: Be careful so that you may make firm your calling and election.

168. 1 John 1:5-10; 2:1-2: If we confess our sins, he is faithful and just and will forgive our sins and cleanse us from all injustice.

169. John 2:3-11: Whoever hates his brother remains in darkness.

170. 1 John 3:1-24: We know that we have crossed over from death to life because we love our brothers.

171. 1 John 4:16-21: God is love and he who lives in love, lives in God, and God in him.

172. Revelation 2:1-5: Do penance and return to your former ways.

173. Revelation 3:14-22: Because you are lukewarm, neither hot or cold, I will vomit you out of my mouth.

174. Revelation 20:11-15: All have been judged according to their works.

175. Revelation 21:1-8: Whoever conquers will inherit all this, and I will be his God, and he will be my son.

176. Matthew 3:1-12: Repent, for the kingdom of heaven is close at hand.

177. Matthew 4:12-17: Repent, for the kingdom of heaven is close at hand.

178. Matthew 5:1-12: When he saw the crowds, he went up to the hill and taught his disciples.

179. Matthew 5:13-16: Let your light shine before men.

180. Matthew 5:17-47: But I am speaking to you.

181. Matthew 9:1-8: Have confidence, my son, your sins are forgiven.

182. Matthew 9:9-13: I did not come to call the just, but sinners.

183. Matthew 18:15-20: You have won back your brother.

184. Matthew 18:21-35: This is the way my heavenly Father will deal with you unless each one forgives his brother from his heart.

185. Matthew 25:31-46: Whatever you have done to the very least of my brothers, you have done to me.

186. Matthew 26:69-75: Peter went outside and wept bitterly.

187. Mark 12:28-34: This is the first commandment.

188. Luke 7:36-50: Her many sins must have been forgiven her, because she loved much.

189. Luke 13:1-5: Unless you repent you will all perish as they did.

190. Luke 15:1-10: Heaven is filled with joy when one sinner turns back to God.

191. Luke 15:11-32: When he was still far away, his father saw him and was moved with mercy. He ran to him and embraced and kissed him.

192. Luke 17:1-6: If your brother sins against you seven times a day and returns to you seven times a day and says I am sorry, you must forgive him.

193. Luke 18:9-14: God, be merciful to me, a sinner.

194. Luke 19:1-10: The Son of Man has come to seek out and save what was lost.

195. Luke 23:39-43: Today you will be with me in paradise.

196. John 8:1-11: Go and sin no more.

197. John 8:31-36: Everyone who commits sin is a slave of sin.

198. John 15:1-8: The Father prunes every barren branch, and every branch that bears fruit he makes it bear even more.

199. John 15:9-14: You are my friends if you do what I command you.

200. John 19:13-37: They shall look on him whom they pierced.

201. John 20:19-23: Receive the Holy Spirit; whose sins you forgive, they are forgiven.

INVITATION OF THE MINISTER FOR THE GENERAL CONFESSION OF SINS

If the prayer is directed to the Father:

202.

Dear friends in Christ, our merciful Father does not desire the death of the sinner but rather that he should turn back to him and have life. Let us pray that we who are sorry for our past sins may fear no future evil and sin no more.

℞. Spare us, Lord; spare your people.

Or:

God who is infinitely merciful pardons all who are repentant and takes away their guilt. Confident in his goodness, let us ask him to forgive all our sins as we confess them with sincerity of heart.

℞. Lord, hear our prayer.

Or:

God gave us his Son for our sins and raised him up to make us holy. Let us humbly pray to the Father.

℞. Lord, have mercy on your people.

Or:

God our Father waits for the return of those who are lost and welcomes them back as his children. Let us pray that we may turn back to him and be received with kindness into his house.

℞. Lord, do not hold our sins against us.

Or:

Father, we have sinned in your sight; we are unworthy to be called your children.

Or:

Our God seeks out what is lost, leads home the abandoned, binds up what is broken and gives strength to the weak; let us ask him to help us.

℞. Lord, heal our weakness.

203.

> Jesus Christ is the victor over sin and death: in his mercy may he pardon our offenses against God and reconcile us with the Church we have wounded by our sins.
>
> ℟. Lord Jesus, be our salvation.

Or:

> In his great love Christ willingly suffered and died for our sins and for the sins of all mankind. Let us come before him with faith and hope to pray for the salvation of the world.
>
> ℟. Christ, graciously hear us.

Or:

> Let us pray with confidence to Christ, the Good Shepherd, who seeks out the lost sheep and carries it back with joy.
>
> ℟. Lord, seek us out and bring us home.

Or:

> Christ our Lord bore our sins upon the cross and by his suffering has brought us healing, so that we live for God and are dead to sin. Let us pray with humility and trust.
>
> ℟. Lord, to whom shall we go? You have the words of eternal life. We have come to believe and to know that you are the Christ, the Son of God.
>
> Or:
>
> Have pity on us, and help us.

Or:

> Christ our Lord was given up to death for our sins and rose again for our justification. Let us pray to him with confidence in his goodness.
>
> ℟. You are our Savior.
>
> Or:
>
> Jesus Christ, Son of the living God, have pity on us.

PENITENTIAL INTERCESSIONS

(At least one of the intercessions should always be a petition for a true conversion of heart.)

If the prayer is addressed to the Father:

204.

By human weakness we have disfigured the holiness of the Church: pardon all our sins and restore us to full communion with our brethren.

℟.   Lord, hear our prayer.   Or: Lord, hear us.

(Or another suitable response may be used.)

Your mercy is our hope: welcome us to the sacrament of reconciliation.   ℟.

Give us the will to change our lives, and the lives of others, by charity, good example and prayer.   ℟.

As we make our confession, rescue us from slavery to sin and lead us to the freedom enjoyed by your children.   ℟.

Make us a living sign of your love for all to see: people reconciled with you and with each other.   ℟

Through the sacrament of reconciliation may we grow in your peace and seek to spread it throughout the world.   ℟

In this sign of your love you forgive us our sins: may it teach us to love others and to forgive their sins against us.   ℟.

In your mercy clothe us in the wedding garment of grace and welcome us to your table.   ℟.

Forgive us our sins, lead us in the ways of goodness and love, and bring us to the reward of everlasting peace.   ℟.

Give light to our darkness and lead us by your truth.   ℟.

In justice you punish us: in your mercy set us free for the glory of your name.   ℟.

May your power keep safe from all danger those whom your love sets free from the chains of sin.   ℟.

Look on our weakness: do not be angry and condemn, but in your love cleanse, guide and save us.   ℟.

In your mercy free us from the past and enable us to begin a new life of holiness.   ℟.

When we stray from you, guide us back into the way of holiness, love and peace. ℟.

By your redeeming love overcome our sinfulness and the harm it has brought us. ℟.

Blot out the sins of the past and fit us for the life that is to come. ℟.

Or:

The following intercessions may be used with a variable response or with an invariable response as in the *Liturgy of the Hours.*

In your goodness forgive our sins against the unity of your family,
—make us one in heart, one in spirit.

We have sinned, Lord, we have sinned,
—take away our sins by your saving grace.

Give us pardon for our sins,
—and reconciliation with your Church.

Touch our hearts and change our lives, make us grow always in your friendship,
—help us to make up for our sins against your wisdom and goodness.

Cleanse and renew your Church, Lord,
—may it grow in strength as a witness to you.

Touch the hearts of those who have abandoned you through sin and scandal,
—call them back to you and keep them faithful in your love.

May we show forth in our lives the sufferings of your Son,
—you raised us up to life when you raised him from the dead.

Have mercy on us, Lord, as we praise and thank you,
—with your pardon give us also your peace.

Lord, our sins are many, but we trust in your mercy,
—call us, and we shall turn to you.

Receive us as we come before you with humble and contrite hearts,
—those who trust in you shall never trust in vain.

We have turned away from you and fallen into sin,
—we have followed evil ways and rejected your commandments.

Turn to us, Lord, and show us your mercy; blot out our sins,
—cast them into the depths of the sea.

Restore us, Lord, to your favor, and give us joy in your presence,
—may our glory be to serve you with all our hearts.

If the prayer is addressed to Christ:

205.

By your death you reconciled us with the Father and brought us salvation. (Romans 5:10)

℟. Lord, have mercy. Or: Christ, hear us.

(Or another suitable response may be used.)

You died and rose again, and sit at the right hand of the Father, to make intercession for us. ℟. (Romans 8:34)

You came from God as our wisdom and justice, our sanctification and redemption. ℟. (1 Corinthians 1:30)

You washed mankind in the Spirit of our God; you made us holy and righteous. ℟. (1 Corinthians 6:11)

You warned us that if we sin against each other we sin against you. ℟. (1 Corinthians 8:12)

Though you were rich you became poor for our sake, so that by your poverty we might become rich. ℟. (2 Corinthians 8:9)

You gave yourself up for our sins to save us from this evil world. ℟. (Galatians 1:4)

You rose from the dead to save us from the anger that was to come. ℟. (1 Thessalonians 1:10)

You came into the world to save sinners. ℟. (1 Timothy 1:15)

You gave yourself up to bring redemption to all. ℟. (1 Timothy 2:6)

You destroyed death and gave light to life. ℟. (2 Timothy 1:10)

You will come to judge the living and the dead. ℟. (2 Timothy 4:1)

You gave yourself up for us to redeem us from all sin and to prepare for yourself a holy people, marked as your own, devoted to good works. ℟. (Titus 2:14)

You showed us your mercy, and as a faithful high priest in the things of God you made atonement for the sins of the people. ℟.   (Hebrews 2:17)

You became the source of salvation for all who obey you. ℟.
                                                 (Hebrews 5:9)

Through the Holy Spirit you offered yourself to God as a spotless victim, cleansing our consciences from lifeless works. ℟.
                                                 (Hebrews 9:15)

You were offered in sacrifice to undo the sins of the many. ℟.
                                                 (Hebrews 9:28)

Once and for all you died for our sins, the innocent one for the guilty. ℟.   (1 Peter 3:18)

You are the atonement for our sins and for the sins of the world. ℟.   (1 John 2:2)

You died that those who believe in you may not perish but have eternal life. ℟.   (John 3:16, 35)

You came into the world to seek and save what was lost. ℟.
                                                 (Matthew 18:11)

You were sent by the Father, not to judge the world but to save it. ℟.   (John 3:17)

You have power on earth to forgive sins. ℟.   (Mark 2:10)

You invite all who labor and are burdened to come to you to be refreshed. ℟.   (Matthew 11:28)

You gave your apostles the keys of the kingdom of heaven, the power to bind and to loose. ℟.   (Matthew 16:19; 18:18)

You told us that the whole law depends on love of God and of our neighbor. ℟.   (Matthew 22:38-40)

Jesus, life of all mankind, you came into the world to give us life, life in its fullness. ℟.   (John 10:10)

Jesus, Good Shepherd, you gave your life for your sheep. ℟.
                                                 (John 10:11)

Jesus, eternal truth, you give us true freedom. ℟.
                                           (John 14:6; 8:32, 36)

Jesus, you are the way to the Father. ℟.   (John 14:6)

Jesus, you are the resurrection and life; those who believe in you, even if they are dead, will live. ℟.   (John 11:25)

Jesus, true vine, the Father prunes your branches to make them bear even greater fruit. ℟. (John 15:1-2)

Or:

The following intercessions may be used with a variable response or with an invariable response as in the *Liturgy of the Hours*.

Healer of body and soul, bind up the wounds of our hearts,
—that our lives may grow strong through grace.

Help us to strip ourselves of sin,
—and put on the new life of grace.

Redeemer of the world, give us the spirit of penance and a deeper devotion to your passion,
—so that we may have a fuller share in your risen glory.

May your Mother, the refuge of sinners, intercede for us,
—and ask you in your goodness to pardon our sins.

You forgave the woman who repented,
—show us also your mercy.

You brought back the lost sheep on your shoulders,
—pity us and lead us home.

You promised paradise to the good thief,
—take us with you into your Kingdom.

You died for us and rose again,
—make us share in your death and resurrection.

PROCLAMATION OF PRAISE

206.

Psalm 31:1-7, 10-11
 ℞. Rejoice in the Lord and sing for joy, friends of God.

Psalm 98:1-9
 ℞. The Lord has remembered his mercy.

Psalm 100:2-5
 ℞. The Lord is loving and kind: his mercy is for ever.

Psalm 119:1, 10-13, 15-16, 18, 33, 105, 169, 170, 174-175
 ℞. Blessed are you, Lord; teach me your decrees.

Psalm 103:1-4, 8-18
 ℞. The mercy of the Lord is from everlasting to everlasting on those who revere him.

Psalm 145:1-21
 ℞. Day after day I will bless you, Lord: I will praise your name for ever.

Psalm 146:2-10
 ℞. I will sing to my God all the days of my life.

Isaiah 12:1b-6
 ℞. Praise the Lord and call upon his name.

Isaiah 61:10-11
 ℞. My spirit rejoices in my God.

Jeremiah 31:10-14
 ℞. The Lord has redeemed his people.

Daniel 3:52-57
 ℞. Bless the Lord, all the works of his hand: praise and glorify him for ever.

Luke 1:46-55
 ℞. The Lord has remembered his mercy.

Ephesians 1:3-10
 ℞. Blessed be God who chose us in Christ.

Revelation 15:3-4
 ℞. Great and wonderful are all your works, Lord.

CONCLUDING PRAYERS

207. Father, all-powerful and ever-living God,
we do well always and everywhere to give you thanks.

When you punish us, you show your justice;
when you pardon us, you show your kindness;
yet always your mercy enfolds us.

When you chastise us, you do not wish to condemn us;
when you spare us, you give us time to make amends
   for our sins
through Christ our Lord.

R̞. Amen.

208. Lord God,
creator and ruler of your kingdom of light,
in your great love for this world
you gave up your only Son
for our salvation.
His cross has redeemed us,
his death has given us life,
his resurrection has raised us to glory.
Through him we ask you
to be always present among your family.
Teach us to be reverent in the presence of your glory;
fill our hearts with faith,
our days with good works,
our lives with your love;
may your truth be on our lips
and your wisdom in all our actions,
that we may receive the reward of everlasting life.

We ask this through Christ our Lord.

R̞. Amen.

209. Lord Jesus Christ,
your loving forgiveness knows no limits.
You took our human nature
to give us an example of humility
and to make us faithful in every trial.

May we never lose the gifts you have given us,
but if we fall into sin
lift us up by your gift of repentance,
for you live and reign for ever and ever.

℞. Amen.

210. Father,
in your love you have brought us
from evil to good and from misery to happiness.
Through your blessings
give the courage of perseverance
to those you have called and justified by faith.

Grant this through Christ our Lord.

℞. Amen.

211. God and Father of us all,
you have forgiven our sins
and sent us your peace.
Help us to forgive each other
and to work together to establish peace in
the world.

We ask this through Christ our Lord.

℞. Amen.

212. And may the blessing of almighty God,
the Father, and the Son, ✠ and the Holy Spirit,
come upon you and remain with you for ever.

℞. Amen.

213. May the Father bless us,
for we are his children, born to eternal life.

℞. Amen.

May the Son show us his saving power,
for he died and rose for us.

℞. Amen.

May the Spirit give us his gift of holiness
and lead us by the right path,
for he dwells in our hearts.

℞. Amen.

214. May the Father bless us,
for he has adopted us as his children.

℟. Amen.

May the Son come to help us,
for he has received us as brothers and sisters.

℟. Amen.

May the Spirit be with us,
for he has made us his dwelling place.

℟. Amen.

APPENDIX I

ABSOLUTION FROM CENSURES

1. The form of absolution is not to be changed in respect to sins which are now reserved either in themselves or by reason of a censure. It is enough that the confessor intend to absolve the properly disposed penitent from these reserved sins. Until other provision is made and as may be necessary, the present regulations which make recourse to the competent authority obligatory are to be observed. Before absolving from sins, however, the confessor may absolve from the censure, using the formula which is given below for absolution from censure outside the sacrament of penance.

2. When a priest, in accordance with the law, absolves a penitent from a censure outside the sacrament of penance, he uses the following formula:

By the power granted to me,
I absolve you
from the bond of excommunication
    (or suspension or interdict).
In the name of the Father, and of the Son, ✠
and of the Holy Spirit.

℞. **Amen.**

DISPENSATION FROM IRREGULARITY

3. When, in accordance with the law, a priest dispenses a penitent from an irregularity, either during confession, after absolution has been given, or outside the sacrament of penance, he says:

By the power granted to me
I dispense you from the irregularity
which you have incurred.
In the name of the Father, and of the Son, ✠
and of the Holy Spirit.

℞. **Amen.**

APPENDIX II

SAMPLE PENITENTIAL SERVICES

These services have been prepared by the Congregation for Divine Worship to help those who prepare or lead penitential celebrations.

PREPARING PENITENTIAL CELEBRATIONS

1.   Penitential celebrations, mentioned in the Rite of Penance (nos. 36-37), are beneficial in fostering the spirit and virtue of penance among individuals and communities; they also help in preparing for a more fruitful celebration of the sacrament of penance. However, the faithful must be reminded of the difference between these celebrations and sacramental confession and absolution.[1]

2.   The particular conditions of life, the manner of speaking, and the educational level of the congregation or special group should be taken into consideration. Thus liturgical commissions [2] and individual Christian communities preparing these celebrations should choose the texts and format most suited to the circumstances of each particular group.

3.   To this end, several examples of penitential celebrations are given below. These are models and should be adapted to the specific conditions and needs of each community.

4.   When the sacrament of penance is celebrated in these services, it follows the readings and homily, and the rite of reconciling several penitents with individual confession and absolution is used (nos. 54-59, Rite of Penance); when permitted by law, the rite for general confession and absolution is used (nos. 60-63, Rite of Penance).

I. PENITENTIAL CELEBRATIONS DURING LENT

5.   Lent is the principal time of penance both for individual Christians and for the whole Church. It is therefore desirable to prepare the

---

[1] See Congregation for the Doctrine of the Faith, *Normae pastorales circa absolutionem sacramentalem generali modo impertiendam*, June 16, 1972, no. X: AAS 64 (1972) 513.

[2] See Congregation of Rites, Instruction *Inter Oecumenici*, September 26, 1964, no. 39: AAS (1964) 110.

Christian community for a fuller sharing in the paschal mystery by penitential celebrations during Lent.[1]

6.   Texts from the lectionary and sacramentary may be used in these penitential celebrations; the penitential nature of the liturgy of the word in the Masses for Lent should be considered.

7.   Two outlines of penitential celebrations suitable for Lent are given here. The first emphasizes penance as strengthening or restoring baptismal grace; the second shows penance as a preparation for a fuller sharing in the Easter mystery of Christ and his Church.

FIRST EXAMPLE: PENANCE LEADS TO A STRENGTHENING OF BAPTISMAL GRACE

8.   a) After an appropriate song and the greeting by the minister, the meaning of this celebration is explained to the people. It prepares the Christian community to recall their baptismal grace at the Easter Vigil and to reach newness of life in Christ through freedom from sins.

Prayer

9.   b)

My brothers and sisters, we have neglected the gifts of our baptism and fallen into sin. Let us ask God to renew his grace within us as we turn to him in repentance.

Let us kneel (or: **Bow your heads before God).**

All pray in silence for a brief period.

Let us stand (or: **Raise your heads).**

Lord Jesus,
you redeemed us by your passion
and raised us to new life in baptism.
Protect us with your unchanging love
and share with us the joy of your resurrection,
for you live and reign for ever and ever.

℞.   **Amen.**

Readings

10.   c)

First Reading
1 Corinthians 10:1-13: All this that happened to the people of Moses in the desert was written for our benefit.

---

[1] See Second Vatican Council, constitution *Sacrosanctum Concilium*, no. 109; Paul VI, Apostolic Constitution *Paenitemini*, February 17, 1966, no. IX: AAS 58 (1966) 185.

Responsorial Psalm
Psalm 106:6-10, 13-14, 19-22

℟ (4): **Lord, remember us,**
for the love you bear your people.

Gospel

Luke 15:4-7: Share my joy: I have found my lost sheep.
or Luke 15:11-32: Your brother here was dead, and has come to life.

Homily

11. d)

The celebrant may speak about:

—the need to fulfill the grace of baptism by living faithfully the Gospel of Christ (see 1 Corinthians 10:1-13);

—the seriousness of sin committed after baptism (see Hebrews 6:4-8);

—the unlimited mercy of our God and Father who continually welcomes those who turn back to him after having sinned (see Luke 15);

—Easter as the feast when the Church rejoices over the Christian initiation of catechumens and the reconciliation of penitents.

Examination of conscience

12. e)

After the homily, the examination of conscience takes place; a sample text is given in Appendix III, page 111. A period of silence should always be included so that each person may personally examine his conscience. In a special way the people should examine their conscience on the baptismal promises which will be renewed at the Easter Vigil.

Act of repentance

13. f)

The deacon (or another minister, if there is no deacon) speaks to the assembly:

My brothers and sisters, the hour of God's favor draws near, the day of his mercy and of our salvation, when death was destroyed and eternal life began. This is the season for planting new vines in God's vineyard, the time for pruning the vines to ensure a richer harvest.

We all acknowledge that we are sinners. We are moved to penance, encouraged by the example and prayers of our brothers and sisters. We admit our guilt and say: "Lord, I acknowledge my sins; my offenses are always before me. Turn away your

83

face, Lord, from my sins, and blot out all my wrong-doing. Give me back the joy of your salvation and give me a new and steadfast spirit."

We are sorry for having offended God by our sins. May he be merciful and hear us as we ask to be restored to his friendship and numbered among the living who share the joy of Christ's risen life.

Then the priest sprinkles the congregation with holy water, while all sing (say):

Cleanse us, Lord, from all our sins;
Wash us, and we shall be whiter than snow.

Then the priest says:

Lord our God,
you created us in love
and redeemed us in mercy.
While we were exiled from heaven
by the jealousy of the evil one,
you gave us your only Son,
who shed his blood to save us.
Send now your Holy Spirit
to breathe new life into your children,
for you do not want us to die
but to live for you alone.
You do not abandon those who abandon you;
correct us as a Father
and restore us to your family.

Lord,
your sons and daughters stand before you
in humility and trust.
Look with compassion on us
as we confess our sins.
Heal our wounds;
stretch out a hand of pity
to save us and raise us up.
Keep us free from harm
as members of Christ's body,
as sheep of your flock,
as children of your family.
Do not allow the enemy
to triumph over us

or death to claim us for ever,
for you raised us to new life in baptism.

Hear, Lord, the prayers we offer from contrite hearts.
Have pity on us as we acknowledge our sins.
Lead us back to the way of holiness.
Protect us now and always
from the wounds of sin.
May we ever keep safe in all its fullness
the gift your love once gave us
and your mercy now restores.

We ask this through our Lord Jesus Christ, your Son,
who lives and reigns with you and the Holy Spirit,
one God for ever and ever.

℞.   Amen.

The celebration ends with an appropriate song and the dismissal of
the people.

**SECOND EXAMPLE: PENANCE PREPARES FOR A FULLER SHARING IN THE
PASCHAL MYSTERY OF CHRIST FOR THE SALVATION OF THE WORLD**

14.   a) After an appropriate song and the greeting by the minister, the
faithful are briefly reminded that they are linked with each other in sin
and in repentance so that each should take his calling to conversion as
an occasion of grace for the whole community.

Prayer

15.   b)

My brothers and sisters, let us pray that by penance we may be
united with Christ, who was crucified for our sins, and so share
with all mankind in his resurrection.

Let us kneel (or: Bow your heads before God).

All pray in silence for a brief period.

Let us stand (or: Raise your heads).

Lord, our God and Father,
through the passion of your Son
you gave us new life.
By our practice of penance
make us one with him in his dying
so that we and all mankind

85

may be one with him
in his resurrection.

We ask this through Christ our Lord.

℞. **Amen.**

Or:

**Almighty and merciful Father,
send your Holy Spirit
to inspire and strengthen us,
so that by always carrying
the death of Jesus in our bodies
we may also show forth the power of his
    risen life.**

We ask this through Christ our Lord.

℞. **Amen.**

Readings

16.   c)

First Reading
Isaiah 53:1-7, 10-12: He is the one who bore our sufferings.

Responsorial Psalm
Psalm 23:2-3, 7-9, 18-28

Second Reading
1 Peter 2:20-25: You had gone astray but now you have come back to the shepherd and guardian of your souls.

Gospel

Verse before the gospel

Glory to you, Lord; you were given up to death for our sins and rose again for our justification. Glory to you, Lord.

Or an appropriate song may be sung.

Mark 10:32-45 (or short form: Mark 10:32-34, 42-45)
Now we are going up to Jerusalem, and the Son of Man will be handed over.

Homily

17.   d)

The celebrant may speak about:

—sin, by which we offend God and also Christ's body, the Church, whose members we became in baptism;

—sin as a failure of love for Christ who in the paschal mystery showed his love for us to the end;

—the way we affect each other when we do good or choose evil;

—the mystery of vicarious satisfaction by which Christ bore the burden of our sins, so that by his wounds we would be healed (see Isaiah 53; 1 Peter 2:24);

—the social and ecclesial dimension of penance by which individual Christians share in the work of converting the whole community;

—the celebration of Easter as the feast of the Christian community which is renewing itself by the conversion or repentance of each member, so that the Church may become a clearer sign of salvation in the world.

Examination of conscience

18.　e)

After the homily, the examination of conscience takes place; a sample text is given in Appendix III, page 111. A period of silence should always be included so that each person may personally examine his conscience.

Act of repentance

19.　f)

After the examination of conscience, all say together:

I confess to almighty God,
and to you, my brothers and sisters,
that I have sinned through my own fault

They strike their breast:

in my thoughts and in my words,
in what I have done,
and in what I have failed to do;
and I ask blessed Mary, ever virgin,
all the angels and saints,
and you, my brothers and sisters,
to pray for me to the Lord our God.

As a sign of conversion and charity toward others, it should be suggested that the faithful give something to help the poor to celebrate the feast of Easter with joy; or they might visit the sick, or make up for some injustice in the community, or perform similar works.

Then the Lord's Prayer may be said, which the priest concludes in this way:

Deliver us, Father, from every evil
as we unite ourselves through penance
with the saving passion of your Son.

Grant us a share
in the joy of the resurrection of Jesus
who is Lord for ever and ever.

℟. Amen.

Depending on circumstances, the general confession may be followed by a form of devotion such as adoration of the cross or the way of the cross, according to local customs and the wishes of the people.

At the end, an appropriate song is sung, and the people are sent away with a greeting or blessing.

II. PENITENTIAL CELEBRATIONS DURING ADVENT

20.   a) After an appropriate song and the greeting by the minister, the meaning of the celebration is explained in these or similar words:

My brothers and sisters, Advent is a time of preparation, when we make ready to celebrate the mystery of our Lord's coming as man, the beginning of our redemption. Advent also moves us to look forward with renewed hope to the second coming of Christ, when God's plan of salvation will be brought to fulfillment. We are reminded too of our Lord's coming to each one of us at the hour of our death. We must make sure that he will find us prepared for his coming, as the gospel tells us: "Blessed are those servants who are found awake when the Lord comes" (Luke 12:37). This service of penance is meant to make us ready in mind and heart for the coming of Christ, which we are soon to celebrate in the Mass of Christmas.

Or:

Now it is time for you to wake from sleep, for our salvation is nearer to us than it was when we first believed. The night is ending; the day draws near. Let us then cast off the deeds of darkness and put on the armor of light. Let us live honestly as people do in the daylight, not in carousing and drunkenness, not in lust and debauchery, not in quarreling and jealousy. But rather let us put on the Lord Jesus Christ and give no thought to the desires of the flesh.

(Romans 13:11-12)

Prayer

21.   b)

My brothers and sisters, we look forward to celebrating the mystery of Christ's coming on the feast of Christmas. Let us pray that when he comes he may find us awake and ready to receive him.

88

All pray in silence for a brief period.

Lord our God,
maker of the heavens,
as we look forward to the coming of our redeemer
grant us the forgiveness of our sins.

We ask this through Christ our Lord.

℟. **Amen.**

Or:

Eternal Son of God,
creator of the human family
and our redeemer,
come at last among us
as the child of the immaculate Virgin,
and redeem the world.
Reveal your loving presence
by which you set us free from sin
in becoming one like us
in all things but sin,
for you live and reign for ever and ever.

℟. **Amen.**

Readings

22.   c)

First Reading
Malachi 3:1-7a: The Lord whom you seek will come to his temple.

Responsorial Psalm
Psalm 86:1-13

℟. (8)   **Lord, let us see your kindness, and grant us your**
salvation.

Second Reading
Revelation 21:1-12: He will wipe away all the tears from their eyes.

Gospel

Verse before the gospel

I am coming quickly, says the Lord, and I will repay each man.
Come, Lord Jesus.

Or:

The Spirit and the Bride say: "Come."
Let all who hear answer: "Come."
Come, Lord Jesus.

89

Or another appropriate song may be sung.

Matthew 3:1-12: Repent, for the kingdom of heaven is close at hand.

Or:

Luke 3:3-17: All mankind shall see the salvation of God.

Examination of conscience

23. d)

After the homily, the examination of conscience takes place; a sample text is given in Appendix III, page 111. A period of silence should always be included so that each person may personally examine his conscience.

Act of repentance

24. e)

The act of repentance follows the examination of conscience. All may say the *I confess to almighty God* or the intercessions as in no. 60.

The Lord's Prayer is said or sung, and is concluded by the presiding minister in this way:

**Lord our God,
on the first day of creation
you made the light
that scatters all darkness.
Let Christ, the light of lights,
hidden from all eternity,
shine at last on your people
and free us from the darkness of sin.
Fill our lives with good works
as we go out to meet your Son,
so that we may give him a fitting welcome.**

We ask this through Christ our Lord.

℞. **Amen.**

Or:

**Almighty and eternal God,
you sent your only-begotten Son
to reconcile the world to yourself.
Lift from our hearts
the oppressive gloom of sin,
so that we may celebrate
the approaching dawn of Christ's birth
with fitting joy.**

We ask this through Christ our Lord.

℟. **Amen.**

At the end, a song is sung, and the people are sent away with a greeting or blessing.

III. COMMON PENITENTIAL CELEBRATIONS

I. SIN AND CONVERSION

Prayer

25. a)

After an appropriate song (for example, Psalm 139:1-12, 16, 23-24) and greeting, the minister who presides briefly explains the meaning of the readings. Then he invites all to pray. After a period of silence, he concludes the prayer in this way:

Lord Jesus,
you turned and looked on Peter
when he denied you for the third time.
He wept for his sin
and turned again to you in sincere repentance.
Look now on us and touch our hearts,
so that we also may turn back to you
and be always faithful in serving you,
for you live and reign for ever and ever.

℟. **Amen.**

Readings

26. b)

First Reading
Luke 22:31-34: I tell you, Peter: the cock will not crow today before you deny me three times.

A short period of silence follows the reading.

Second Reading
Luke 22:54-62: Peter went out and wept bitterly.

Responsorial Psalm
Psalm 32:10, 15-17, 20 or Psalm 52 or another appropriate song.

Gospel
John 21:15-19: Simon, son of John, do you love me?

Homily

27. c)

The celebrant may speak about:

—the trust we must put in God's grace, not in our own powers;

—the faithfulness by which we as baptized Christians must live as true and faithful followers of the Lord;

—our weakness by which we often fall into sin and refuse to give witness to the gospel;

—the mercy of the Lord, who welcomes as a friend the one who turns to him with his whole heart.

Examination of conscience

28. d)

After the homily, the examination of conscience takes place; a sample text is given in Appendix III, page 111. A period of silence should always be included so that each person may personally examine his conscience.

Act of repentance

29. e)

After the examination of conscience, the presiding minister invites all to prayer in these or similar words:

God gives us an example of love: when we were sinners he first loved us and took pity on us. Let us turn to him with a sincere heart, and in the words of Peter say to him:

℟. **Lord, you know all things; you know that I love you.**

A short period of silence should follow each invocation. Each invocation may be said by different individuals, the rest answering.

Lord, like Peter we have relied on our own strength rather than on grace. Look on us, Lord, and have mercy.

℟. **Lord, you know all things; you know that I love you.**

Our pride and foolishness have led us into temptation. Look on us, Lord, and have mercy.

℟. **Lord, you know all things; you know that I love you.**

We have been vain and self-important. Look on us, Lord, and have mercy.

℟. **Lord, you know all things; you know that I love you.**

We have at times been pleased rather than saddened by the misfortunes of others. Look on us, Lord, and have mercy.

℟. Lord, you know all things; you know that I love you.

We have shown indifference for those in need instead of helping them. Look on us, Lord, and have mercy.

℟. Lord, you know all things; you know that I love you.

We have been afraid to stand up for justice and truth. Look on us, Lord, and have mercy.

℟. Lord, you know all things; you know that I love you.

We have repeatedly broken the promises of our baptism and failed to be your disciples. Look on us, Lord, and have mercy.

℟. Lord, you know all things; you know that I love you.

Let us now pray to the Father in the words Christ gave us and ask forgiveness for our sins:

Our Father . . .

30.   f)

After an appropriate song, the presiding minister says the final prayer and dismisses the people:

Lord Jesus, our Savior,
you called Peter to be an apostle;
when he repented of his sin
you restored him to your friendship
and confirmed him as first of the apostles.
Turn to us with love
and help us to imitate Peter's example.
Give us strength to turn from our sins
and to serve you in the future
with greater love and devotion,
for you live and reign for ever and ever.

℟.   Amen.

II. THE SON RETURNS TO THE FATHER

Prayer

31.   a)

After an appropriate song and the greeting by the minister, the theme of the celebration is explained to the community. Then he invites all to pray. After a period of silence, he says:

Almighty God,
you are the Father of us all.

You created the human family
to dwell for ever with you
and to praise your glory.
Open our ears to hear your voice
so that we may return to you
with sincere repentance for our sins.
Teach us to see in you our loving Father,
full of compassion for all who call to you for help.
We know that you punish us only to set us free from evil
and that you are ready to forgive us our sins.
Restore your gift of salvation
which alone brings true happiness,
so that we may all return to our Father's house
and share your table
now and for ever.

℟. Amen.

Readings

32. b)

First Reading
Ephesians 1:3-7: He chose us from all eternity to be his adopted sons and daughters.

Responsorial Psalm
Psalm 27:1, 4, 7-10, 13-14

Gospel
Luke 15:11-32: His father saw him and was filled with pity.

Homily

33. c)

The minister may speak about:

—sin as a turning away from the love that we should have for God our Father;

—the limitless mercy of our Father for his children who have sinned;

—the nature of true conversion;

—the forgiveness we should extend to our brothers;

—the eucharistic banquet as the culmination of our reconciliation with the Church and with God.

Examination of conscience

34. d)

After the homily, the examination of conscience takes place; a sample text is given in Appendix III, page 111. A period of silence should always be included so that each person may personally examine his conscience.

35.   e)

After the examination of conscience, the presiding minister invites all to pray:

Our God is a God of mercy, slow to anger and full of patience. He is the father who welcomes his son when he returns from a distant country. Let us pray to him with trust in his goodness:

℟.   **We are not worthy to be called your children.**

By our misuse of your gifts we have sinned against you.

℟.   **We are not worthy to be called your children.**

By straying from you in mind and heart we have sinned against you.

℟.   **We are not worthy to be called your children.**

By forgetting your love we have sinned against you.

℟.   **We are not worthy to be called your children.**

By indulging ourselves, while neglecting our true good and the good of our neighbor, we have sinned against you.

℟.   **We are not worthy to be called your children.**

By failing to help our neighbor in his need we have sinned against you.

℟.   **We are not worthy to be called your children.**

By being slow to forgive we have sinned against you.

℟.   **We are not worthy to be called your children.**

By failing to remember your repeated forgiveness we have sinned against you.

℟.   **We are not worthy to be called your children.**

Members of the congregation may add other invocations. A brief period of silence should follow each invocation. It may be desirable to have different individuals say each invocation.

Let us now call upon our Father in the words that Jesus gave us, and ask him to forgive us our sins:

Our Father . . .

36.   f)

After an appropriate song, the presiding minister says the final prayer and dismisses the people:

God our Father,
you chose us to be your children,
to be holy in your sight
and happy in your presence.
Receive us as a loving Father
so that we may share the joy and love
of your holy Church.

We ask this through Christ our Lord.

℞.   Amen.

III. THE BEATITUDES

Prayer

37.   a)

After an appropriate song and greeting of the minister, the person presiding explains briefly the meaning of the readings. Then he invites all to pray. After a period of silence, he says:

Lord,
open our ears and our hearts today
to the message of your Son,
so that through the power of his death and resurrection
we may walk in newness of life.

We ask this through Christ our Lord.

℞.   Amen.

Readings

38.   b)

First Reading
1 John 1:5-9: If we say that we have no sin, we are deceiving ourselves.

Responsorial Psalm
Psalm 146:5-10

Gospel
Matthew 5:1-10: Happy are the poor in spirit, for theirs is the kingdom of heaven.

Homily

39. c)

The minister may speak about:

—sin, by which we ignore the commandments of Christ and act contrary to the teaching of the beatitudes;

—the firmness of our faith in the words of Jesus;

—our faithfulness in imitating Christ in our private lives, in the Christian community, and in human society;

—each beatitude.

Examination of conscience

40. d)

After the homily, the examination of conscience takes place; a sample text is given in Appendix III, page 111. A period of silence should always be included so that each person may personally examine his conscience.

Act of repentance

41. e)

After the examination of conscience, the presiding minister invites all to pray in these or similar words:

My brothers and sisters, Jesus Christ has left an example for us to follow. Humbly and confidently let us ask him to renew us in spirit so that we may shape our lives according to the teaching of his Gospel.

**—Lord Jesus Christ, you said:
"Blessed are the poor in spirit,
for theirs is the kingdom of heaven."
Yet we are preoccupied with money and worldly goods
and even try to increase them at the expense of justice.
Lamb of God, you take away the sin of the world:**

℞. Have mercy on us.

**—Lord Jesus Christ, you said:
"Blessed are the gentle,
for they shall inherit the earth."**

Yet we are ruthless with each other,
and our world is full of discord and violence.
Lamb of God, you take away the sin of the world:

℞. Have mercy on us.

—Lord Jesus Christ, you said:
"Blessed are those who mourn,
for they shall be comforted."
Yet we are impatient under our own burdens
and unconcerned about the burdens of others.
Lamb of God, you take away the sin of the world:

℞. Have mercy on us.

—Lord Jesus Christ, you said:
"Blessed are those who hunger and thirst for justice,
for they shall be filled."
Yet we do not thirst for you, the fountain of all holiness,
and are slow to spread your influence
in our private lives or in society.
Lamb of God, you take away the sin of the world:

℞. Have mercy on us.

—Lord Jesus Christ, you said:
"Blessed are the merciful,
for they shall receive mercy."
Yet we are slow to forgive
and quick to condemn.
Lamb of God, you take away the sin of the world:

℞. Have mercy on us.

—Lord Jesus Christ, you said:
"Blessed are the clean of heart,
for they shall see God."
Yet we are prisoners of our senses and evil desires
and dare not raise our eyes to you.
Lamb of God, you take away the sin of the world:

℞. Have mercy on us.

—Lord Jesus Christ, you said:
"Blessed are the peacemakers,
for they shall be called children of God."
Yet we fail to make peace in our families,
in our country, and in the world.

Lamb of God, you take away the sin of the world:

℟.   **Have mercy on us.**

—**Lord Jesus Christ, you said:**
"Blessed are those who are persecuted
for the sake of justice,
for the kingdom of heaven is theirs."
Yet we prefer to practice injustice
rather than suffer for the sake of right;
we discriminate against our neighbors
and oppress and persecute them.
Lamb of God, you take away the sin of the world:

℟.   **Have mercy on us.**

—**Now let us turn to God our Father and ask him to free**
us from evil and prepare us for the coming of his kingdom:

Our Father . . .

42.   f)

After an appropriate song, the presiding minister says the final prayer and dismisses the people:

Lord Jesus Christ,
gentle and humble of heart,
full of compassion and maker of peace,
you lived in poverty
and were persecuted in the cause of justice.
You chose the cross as the path of glory
to show us the way to salvation.
May we receive with joyful hearts
the word of your Gospel
and live by your example
as heirs and citizens of your kingdom,
where you live and reign for ever and ever.

℟.   **Amen.**

IV. FOR CHILDREN

43.

This service is suitable for younger children, including those who have not yet participated in the sacrament of penance.

THEME: GOD COMES TO LOOK FOR US

44.

The penitential celebration should be prepared with the children so that they will understand its meaning and purpose, be familiar with the songs, have at least an elementary knowledge of the biblical text to be read, and know what they are to say and in what order.

Greeting

45.   a)

When the children have come together in the church or some other suitable place, the celebrant greets them in a friendly manner. Briefly he reminds them why they have come together and recounts the theme of the service. After the greeting, an opening song may be sung.

Reading

46.   b)

The celebrant may give a short introduction to the reading in these or similar words:

> **My dear children, each one of us has been baptized, and so we are all sons and daughters of God. God loves us as a Father, and he asks us to love him with all our hearts. He also wants us to be good to each other, so that we may all live happily together.**

> **But people do not always do what God wants. They say: "I will not obey! I am going to do as I please." They disobey God and do not want to listen to him. We, too, often act like that.**

> **That is what we call sin. When we sin we turn our backs on God. If we do something really bad we cut ourselves off from God; we are complete strangers to him.**

> **What does God do when someone turns away from him? What does he do when we leave the path of goodness that he has shown us, when we run the risk of losing the life of grace he has given us? Does God turn away from us when we turn away from him by our sins?**

> **Here is what God does, in the words of Jesus himself:**

47.

Only one text of Scripture should be read:

Luke 15:1-7: Heaven is filled with joy when one sinner turns back to God.

48. c)

The homily should be short, proclaiming God's love for us and preparing the ground for the examination of conscience.

Examination of conscience

49. d)

The celebrant should adapt the examination to the children's level of understanding by brief comments. There should be a suitable period of silence (see Appendix III, page 111).

Act of repentance

50. e)

This litany may be said by the celebrant or by one or more of the children, alternating with all present. Before the response, which may be sung, all should observe a brief pause.

God our Father,

Sometimes we have not behaved as your children should.

℟.   **But you love us and come to us.**

We have given trouble to our parents and teachers.

℟.   **But you love us and come to us.**

We have quarrelled and called each other names.

℟.   **But you love us and come to us.**

We have been lazy at home and in school, and have not been helpful to our parents (brothers, sisters, friends).

℟.   **But you love us and come to us.**

We have thought too much of ourselves and have told lies.

℟.   **But you love us and come to us.**

We have not done good to others when we had the chance.

℟.   **But you love us and come to us.**

Now with Jesus, our brother, we come before our Father in heaven and ask him to forgive our sins:

Our Father . . .

51. f)

Sorrow may be shown by some sign, for example, individual children may come to the altar or another suitable place with a candle, and light it there; if necessary, a server may help. Each child says in his own words:

Father,
I am sorry for all my sins:
for what I have done
and for what I have failed to do.
I will sincerely try to do better
especially . . . (he mentions his particular resolution)
Help me to walk by your light.

In place of the candle, or in addition to it, the children may prepare a written prayer or resolution and place it on the altar or on a table designated for this purpose.

If the number of children or other circumstances do not allow for this, the celebrant asks the children present to say the above prayer together, along with a general resolution.

Prayer of the celebrant

52. g)

God our Father always seeks us out
when we walk away from the path of goodness.
He is always ready to forgive
when we have sinned.
May almighty God have mercy on us,
forgive us our sins,
and bring us to everlasting life.

℟. **Amen.**

53. The minister invites the children to express their thanks to God. They may do this by an appropriate hymn.
Then he dismisses them.

V. FOR YOUNG PEOPLE

54. The penitential celebration should be prepared with the young people so that with the celebrant, they may choose or compose the texts and songs. The readers, cantors or choir should be chosen from among them.

Greeting

55.   a)

This may be given in these or similar words:

Dear friends, we have come here to do penance and to make a fresh start as Christians. Many people see in penance only its difficult side, and its emphasis on sorrow. But it has also a more joyful side, and it looks more to the future than to the past.

Through penance God calls us to a new beginning. He helps us to find our true freedom as his sons and daughters. When Jesus invites us to repentance, he is inviting us to take our place in his Father's kingdom. This is what he teaches us in the parable about the merchant who came across a pearl of great value and sold everything he had in order to buy it.

If we follow our Lord's advice we exchange our past life for one far more valuable.

Then a song is sung; it should stress the call to a new life or following God's call with an eager heart (for example Psalm 40:1-9. ℟. Here am I, Lord; I come to do your will).

Prayer

56.   b)

Lord our God,
you call us out of darkness into light,
out of self-deception into truth,
out of death into life.
Send us your Holy Spirit
to open our ears to your call.
Fill our hearts with courage
to be true followers of your Son.

We ask this through Christ our Lord.

℟.   Amen.

Readings

57.   c)

First Reading
Romans 7:18-25: Unhappy man am I! Who will free me? Thanks to God through Jesus Christ our Lord.

or: Romans 8:19-23: We know that by turning everything to their good, God cooperates with all those who love him.

A song is sung, or a brief period of silence is observed.

Gospel
Matthew 13:44-46: He sold all that he had and bought the field.

Homily

58. d)

The celebrant may speak about:

—the law of sin which in us struggles against God;

—the necessity of giving up the way of sin so that we may enter the kingdom of God.

Examination of conscience

59. e)

After the homily, the examination of conscience takes place; a sample text is given in Appendix III, page 111. A period of silence should always be included so that each person may personally examine his conscience.

Act of repentance

60. f)

Christ our Lord came to call sinners into his Father's kingdom. Let us now make an act of sorrow in our hearts and resolve to avoid sin in the future.

After a brief period of silence, all say together:

**I confess to almighty God,
and to you, my brothers and sisters,
that I have sinned through my own fault**

They strike their breast:

**in my thoughts and in my words,
in what I have done,
and in what I have failed to do;
and I ask blessed Mary, ever virgin,
all the angels and saints,
and you, my brothers and sisters,
to pray for me to the Lord our God.**

Minister:

**Lord our God,
you know all things.**

**You know that we want to be more generous
in serving you and our neighbor.
Look on us with love and hear our prayer.**

Reader:

Give us the strength to turn away from sin.

℟.   **Hear our prayer.**

Help us to be sorry for our sins and to keep our resolutions.

℟.   **Hear our prayer.**

Forgive our sins and have pity on our weakness.

℟.   **Hear our prayer.**

**Give us trust in your goodness and make us generous in serving
you.**

℟.   **Hear our prayer.**

**Help us to be true followers of your Son and living members of
his Church.**

Minister:

**God does not want the sinner to die, but to turn to him and live.
May he be pleased that we have confessed our sinfulness, and
may he show us his great mercy as we pray in obedience to his
Son.**

All say together:

Our Father . . .

61.   The celebration ends with an appropriate song and the dismissal.

VI. FOR THE SICK

62.   According to the condition of the sick people and the suitability
of the place, the minister goes to the sick, gathered in one room, or else
he brings them together in the sanctuary or church. He should adapt
carefully the texts and their number to the condition of those who
take part in the service. Since in most instances none of the sick will
be able to act as reader, the minister should, if possible, invite another
person to carry out this office.

THEME: THE TIME OF SICKNESS IS A TIME OF GRACE

Greeting

63. a)

He may greet them in these or similar words:

My dear friends, when Jesus came to preach repentance, he was bringing us good news, for he was proclaiming to us God's love and mercy. Again and again God comes to our help so that we may turn to him and live our lives entirely in his service. Penance is his gift, a gift we should accept with gratitude. Keeping this in mind, let us open our hearts to God with great simplicity and humility and ask to be reconciled with him as we now forgive each other.

If possible, a penitential song is sung by the sick persons, or by a choir.

Prayer

64. b)

**Lord our God,
source of all goodness and mercy,
we come together as your family
to ask your forgiveness
and the forgiveness of each other.
Give us true sorrow for our sins
and loving trust in your compassion
so that we may acknowledge our sins
with sincere hearts.
Through this celebration
restore us to fuller union with yourself
and with our neighbor
so that we may serve you with greater generosity.**

We ask this through Christ our Lord.

℟. **Amen.**

Readings

65. c)

The readings may be introduced in these or similar words:

Many people enjoy good health and other blessings and accept them as a matter of course, with no sense of gratitude. In time of sickness we discover that all these are great gifts, and that without them we easily lose heart. God allows us to experience

sickness in order to test our faith. What is more, if we see our suffering as a share in Christ's suffering, it can be of great value both to ourselves and to the Church. The time of sickness is not then wasted or meaningless. It is in fact a time of grace if we accept it as God wants us to accept it. This celebration is meant to help us to do so. We shall therefore listen to God's word, examine our conscience, and pray with sincere hearts.

Readings

66.

James 5:13-16: The prayer of faith will save the sick man.

Responsorial Psalm
Between the readings, a psalm may be said or sung alternately, for ex ample, Psalm 131 or Psalm 52.

Gospel
Mark 2:1-12: The Son of Man has authority on earth to forgive sins.

Homily

67.   d)

It is fitting that the celebrant speak of sickness, dwelling not so much on sickness of the body as on sickness of the soul. He should emphasize the power of Jesus and his Church to forgive sins and the value of suffering offered for others.

Examination of conscience

68.   e)

After the homily, the examination of conscience takes place; a sample text is given in Appendix III, page 111. A period of silence should always be included so that each person may personally examine his conscience.

The following questions may be added but adapted to the condition of the sick:

Do I trust God's goodness and providence, even in times of stress and illness?

Do I give in to sickness, to despair, to other unworthy thoughts and feelings?

Do I fill my empty moments with reflection on life and with prayer to God?

Do I accept my illness and pain as an opportunity for suffering with Christ, who redeemed us by his passion?

Do I live by faith, confident that patience in suffering is of great benefit to the Church?

Am I thoughtful of others and attentive to my fellow patients and their needs?

Am I grateful to those who look after me and visit me?

Do I give a good Christian example to others?

Am I sorry for my past sins, and do I try to make amends for them by my patient acceptance of weakness and illness.

Act of repentance

69.   f)

After a moment of silence, all say together:

I confess to almighty God,
and to you, my brothers and sisters,
that I have sinned through my own fault

They strike their breast:

in my thoughts and in my words,
in what I have done,
and in what I have failed to do;
and I ask blessed Mary, ever virgin,
all the angels and saints,
and you, my brothers and sisters,
to pray for me to the Lord our God.

Reader:

Lord our God, we bear the name of your Son and call you Father. We are sorry for our sins against you and against our brothers and sisters.

R̸.   Give us true repentance and sincere love for you and for our neighbor.

Lord Jesus Christ, you redeemed us by your passion and cross and gave us an example of patience and love. We are sorry for our sins against you, and especially for failing to serve you and our brothers and sisters.

R̸.   Give us true repentance and sincere love for you and for our neighbor.

Holy Spirit, Lord, you speak to us in the Church and in our conscience and inspire within us the desire to do good. We are sorry for our sins against you, and especially for our obstinate refusal to obey you.

R̸.   Give us true repentance and sincere love for you and for our neighbor.

Minister:

Let us ask God our Father to forgive us and to free us from evil:

Our Father . . .

70. Then, if possible, the choir or the assembled people sing a song, and the service concludes with a prayer of thanksgiving:

71.

God of consolation and Father of mercies,
you forgive the sinner who acknowledges his guilt:

℟.   We praise you and thank you.

God of consolation and Father of mercies,
you give to those who suffer hardship or pain
a share in the sufferings of your Son
for the salvation of the world:

℟.   We praise you and thank you.

God of consolation and Father of mercies,
you look with love on those who are troubled or in sorrow;
you give them hope of salvation
and the promise of eternal life:

℟.   We praise you and thank you.

Let us pray.

Lord,
your goodness and mercy are boundless.
Look on your sons and daughters
gathered here in the name of your Son.
We thank you for all your gifts
and ask you to keep us always as your family,
full of living faith, firm hope,
and sincere love for you and for our neighbor.

We ask this through Christ our Lord.

℟.   Amen.

72. In place of the prayer, the service may end with a blessing.

**May the God of peace
fill your hearts with every blessing.
May he sustain you
with his gifts of hope and consolation,
help you to offer your lives in his service,
and bring you safely to eternal glory.
May almighty God,
the Father, and the Son, ✠ and the Holy Spirit,
grant you all that is good.**

℟. **Amen.**

73. The minister dismisses the assembly, or invites those present to a friendly visit with the sick.

APPENDIX III

FORM OF EXAMINATION OF CONSCIENCE

1) This suggested form for an examination of conscience should be completed and adapted to meet the needs of different individuals and to follow local usages.

2) In an examination of conscience, before the sacrament of penance, each individual should ask himself these questions in particular:

1.   What is my attitude to the sacrament of penance? Do I sincerely want to be set free from sin, to turn again to God, to begin a new life, and to enter into a deeper friendship with God? Or do I look on it as a burden, to be undertaken as seldom as possible?

2.   Did I forget to mention, or deliberately conceal, any grave sins in past confessions?

3.   Did I perform the penance I was given? Did I make reparation for any injury to others? Have I tried to put into practice my resolution to lead a better life in keeping with the Gospel?

3) Each individual should examine his life in the light of God's word.

I. **THE LORD SAYS: "YOU SHALL LOVE THE LORD YOUR GOD WITH YOUR WHOLE HEART."**

1.   Is my heart set on God, so that I really love him above all things and am faithful to his commandments, as a son loves his father? Or am I more concerned about the things of this world? Have I a right intention in what I do?

2.   God spoke to us in his Son. Is my faith in God firm and secure? Am I wholehearted in accepting the Church's teaching? Have I been careful to grow in my understanding of the faith, to hear God's word, to listen to instructions on the faith, to avoid dangers to faith? Have I been always strong and fearless in professing my faith in God and the Church? Have I been willing to be known as a Christian in private and public life?

3.   Have I prayed morning and evening? When I pray, do I really raise my mind and heart to God or is it a matter of words only? Do I offer God my difficulties, my joys, and my sorrows? Do I turn to God in time of temptation?

4. Have I love and reverence for God's name? Have I offended him in blasphemy, swearing falsely, or taking his name in vain? Have I shown disrespect for the Blessed Virgin Mary and the saints?

5. Do I keep Sundays and feast days holy by taking a full part, with attention and devotion, in the liturgy, and especially in the Mass? Have I fulfilled the precept of annual confession and of communion during the Easter season?

6. Are there false gods that I worship by giving them greater attention and deeper trust than I give to God: money, superstition, spiritism, or other occult practices?

II. THE LORD SAYS: "LOVE ONE ANOTHER AS I HAVE LOVED YOU."

1. Have I a genuine love for my neighbors? Or do I use them for my own ends, or do to them what I would not want done to myself? Have I given grave scandal by my words or actions?

2. In my family life, have I contributed to the well-being and happiness of the rest of the family by patience and genuine love? Have I been obedient to parents, showing them proper respect and giving them help in their spiritual and material needs? Have I been careful to give a Christian upbringing to my children, and to help them by good example and by exercising authority as a parent? Have I been faithful to my husband (wife) in my heart and in my relations with others?

3. Do I share my possessions with the less fortunate? Do I do my best to help the victims of oppression, misfortune, and poverty? Or do I look down on my neighbor, especially the poor, the sick, the elderly, strangers, and people of other races?

4. Does my life reflect the mission I received in confirmation? Do I share in the apostolic and charitable works of the Church and in the life of my parish? Have I helped to meet the needs of the Church and of the world and prayed for them: for unity in the Church, for the spread of the Gospel among the nations, for peace and justice, etc.?

5. Am I concerned for the good and prosperity of the human community in which I live, or do I spend my life caring only for myself? Do I share to the best of my ability in the work of promoting justice, morality, harmony, and love in human relations? Have I done my duty as a citizen? Have I paid my taxes?

6. In my work or profession am I just, hard-working, honest, serving society out of love for others? Have I paid a fair wage to my employees? Have I been faithful to my promises and contracts?

7. Have I obeyed legitimate authority and given it due respect?

8. If I am in a position of responsibility or authority, do I use this for my own advantage or for the good of others, in a spirit of service?

9. Have I been truthful and fair, or have I injured others by deceit, calumny, detraction, rash judgment, or violation of a secret?

10. Have I done violence to others by damage to life or limb, reputation, honor, or material possessions? Have I involved them in loss? Have I been responsible for advising an abortion or procuring one? Have I kept up hatred for others? Am I estranged from others through quarrels, enmity, insults, anger? Have I been guilty of refusing to testify to the innocence of another because of selfishness?

11. Have I stolen the property of others? Have I desired it unjustly and inordinately? Have I damaged it? Have I made restitution of other people's property and made good their loss?

12. If I have been injured, have I been ready to make peace for the love of Christ and to forgive, or do I harbor hatred and the desire for revenge?

III. CHRIST OUR LORD SAYS: "BE PERFECT AS YOUR FATHER IS PERFECT."

1. Where is my life really leading me? Is the hope of eternal life my inspiration? Have I tried to grow in the life of the Spirit through prayer, reading the word of God and meditating on it, receiving the sacraments, self-denial? Have I been anxious to control my vices, my bad inclinations and passions, e.g., envy, love of food and drink? Have I been proud and boastful, thinking myself better in the sight of God and despising others as less important than myself? Have I imposed my own will on others, without respecting their freedom and rights?

2. What use have I made of time, of health and strength, of the gifts God has given me to be used like the talents in the Gospel? Do I use them to become more perfect every day? Or have I been lazy and too much given to leisure?

3. Have I been patient in accepting the sorrows and disappointments of life? How have I performed mortification so as to "fill up what is wanting to the sufferings of Christ?" Have I kept the precept of fasting and abstinence?

4. Have I kept my senses and my whole body pure and chaste as a temple of the Holy Spirit consecrated for resurrection and glory, and as a sign of God's faithful love for men and women, a sign that is seen most perfectly in the sacrament of matrimony? Have I dishonored my body by fornification, impurity, unworthy conversation or thoughts, evil desires, or actions? Have I given in to sensuality? Have I indulged in reading, conversation, shows, and entertainments that offend against Christian and human decency? Have I encouraged others to sin by my own failure to maintain these standards? Have I been faithful to the moral law in my married life?

5. Have I gone against my conscience out of fear or hypocrisy?

6. Have I always tried to act in the true freedom of the sons of God according to the law of the Spirit, or am I the slave of forces within me?

NOTES

NOTES

NOTES

NOTES

NOTES

STANDING ORDER SERVICE

By filling in and returning the form below, you will be included in the standing order service, a plan by which each new printing of the USCC Publications Office is automatically mailed to subscribers. These printings are mainly Papal Documents and the Bishops' yearly statements but may include special publications or an occasional item of current interest. Many include indexes, study outlines and bibliographies.

Not all Papal messages or documents are included but rather a selection of the more important ones or those of special interest to American Catholics, or for which there is an unusual number of requests.

There are usually from 15 to 30 printings each year ranging in price from 10¢ to 75¢. The total yearly bill is usually $15.00 to $25.00 depending on the number of items published during the year. Occasional special standing order discounts off the list prices are offered on some items.

Billings are made annually in January for the preceding year, unless you specify otherwise or unless the quantity ordered is large. You may cancel your standing order any time.

— —

I wish to place a standing order for .... copies of all new printings issued by the USCC Publications Office until such time as I request cancellation of this order.

Please address the mailings as follows:

Name ....
        (Print)

Address ....

City .... State .... Zip ....

Signature ....